INDIGO
The Search for True Understanding and Balance

©*Copyright by 1999 by Ceanne DeRohan*
All rights reserved. No part of this publication may be produced or transmitted in any form or by any means, electronic or mechanical, including photocopying recording, or any information storage and retrieval system, without the publisher's prior written permission.

For permissions contact:

Four Winds Publications
1000 Cordova Place Suite 112
Santa Fe, New Mexico 87505

Dedicated to

The Four Parts of God
in Loving Balance

INDIGO

The Search for
True Understanding
and Balance

Received by Ceanne DeRohan

FOUR WINDS PUBLICATIONS

TABLE OF CONTENTS

INTRODUCTION i
THE MOTHER AND LOST WILL OF HEART 1
ANOTHER FRIGHTENING LOST WILL
    FRAGMENTATION 7
ANOTHER LOOK AT THE PURPLE GAP 18
PURPLE GAP'S INVOLVEMENT IN THE SPIRITUAL
    PROBLEMS ON EARTH..30
INDIGO AND BLUE 44
RAGE NEEDS MOVEMENT EVEN IN INDIGO...................54
DAUGHTER HEART'S INVOLVEMENT IN THE PURPLE
    GAP 59
THE PLIGHT OF THE INDIGO SEER...................................75
THE DEPARTURE 97
THE ROMANS "TEACH" THE MOTHER HOW SHE IS
    SUPPOSED TO BEHAVE 102
THE MOVEMENT GOES UNDERGROUND 107
THE CONCLUSION OF THE HIGH PRIESTESS'S LIFE AT
    DELPHI..120
THE ISLE 126
THE NEW TEMPLE...137
LOST WILL NEEDS MORE LIGHT
    SOME MORE INFORMATION ON HOW THE GAP
    MOVED DOWN THROUGH THE CHAKRAS 165
HEART ATTEMPTS TO BRIDGE THE GAP IN PURPLE ...173
KING ARTHUR...186
MERLIN AND MORGAN LE FEY 198
MY LIGHT KNOWS THE BALANCE POINT 201
A STATE OF DENIAL THAT NEEDS HELP NOW..............204
CONCLUSION 212

INTRODUCTION

If this is not the first book in the Right Use of Will series that you have picked up, please do not read it unless you know what the gap is, at least some of how and why it happened that way and at least some of what you have had in it. Then, this book can help you understand more. Otherwise, you are not ready for this book, and you will not be helping whatever process you have by reading it.

If this is the first book in the Right Use of Will series that you have picked up, please read all of the other books in the series in order first, because you will not know what I am really saying otherwise, and so this book will not help you in the ways you hope it will. If you go back and read the others first, it will be well worth it to you, because then you will understand so much more when you get to this book than you have in the past, or will, if you try to read it now. To go back and start at the beginning, you need all of the books, of which this is the eighth. In numerology, the number eight is mastery of the physical plane of existence, but it needs to be the mastery of True Understanding and Balance, which cannot be found without alignment of Spirit, Will, Heart and Body. Only this alignment brings true Heart.

Many people think that Spirit, Body and mind are capable of finding True Understanding and Balance, but this is not the case. If you do not already know this, you are not ready for this book. The long, painful and difficult search for True Understanding and Balance has been complicated by denial and almost entirely co-opted into obscurity by point of view. Because of this, most people do not know what true Heart really is or even what the Will is anymore. Most people think the Will is something generated by the mind and controlled by the mind as in positive thinking. This is not the case. This is a dictatorship. True Heart is more than heart coming from the mind or Spirit. Until the Will side of heart is fully felt, understood and integrated, there is no such thing as true Heart in anyone on Earth.

To be ready to read this book, it is necessary to move along with your own Original Cause to know that you have this point of view problem, to know what your point of view is, to be moving your emotions and releasing the judgments/imprints that have held your own point of view in place for so long. It is also important to have been into your gap enough to know what it is and how it has empowered the holding of your own point of view. You can discover your point of view by reading the other books and noticing very closely what your responses are, what they're toward, what they're for and what they're against. It is important to take responsibility, not only for your own victimization, but also your own perpetration and to learn how to realistically widen your own point of view by going into the imprints that have been holding it in place.

Even many of you who have read all of the books and think you are ready for this one are not unless you are moving along well with all of these things and have, at least, begun to recognize what you have denied so heavily that you had not remembered that this is, nonetheless, part of you. The gap needs understanding now. Ceanne's note: I took out of the revised edition of Indigo what was bothering me as just too much, but, I am replacing it now. Uncomfortable as it was making me, as a part of the gap, it has a presence on Earth that is in desperate need of being healed.

If you are taking this path or are going to take this path, be a good reader. Go back over things after you have moved emotion, and see if they have other or deeper meanings than they did the first time or even the first several times you read them. Do not read past or through triggers. Take a break there, and look deeper and feel deeper than you ever have before. Rather than blame the path for your own apparent lack of understanding, welcome every response that surfaces in you and everything that enters your outer awareness as an opportunity to increase the depth and breadth of your perceptions and understandings.

There are many things that are only one line in the books, but focusing on those portals can open vast areas of information and movement to you. Other things are said over and over because it has needed to be said in many different ways and in many different settings, over time, for it to start to penetrate long held points of view and conditioning. Continuing to read when you feel that you are triggered may take you to places where understandings are being given that may lift you out of the emotions that were stirred and allow you to rationalize them away and thus, deny your Will acceptance, participation and opportunity to evolve.

Your lack of understanding may not be very apparent to you, but it is to My Light. I know that this path works, even if it does not seem to be working for you. You need to suspect that every one of your beliefs is quite possibly not all there is to reality. There is so much more to reality than anyone has been able to remain aware of or retain in their memory that it is not even possible to write it into books, but the place to start is to be thorough in the discovery of your own story. As lengthy as these books have gotten to be, it has only been possible to give the most necessary parts of the information on the Main Body experiences along with some information about some of the fragmentation that gave the reflections most needed, but you can find your own story by feeling where you react, where you have involvement and where you may not have even been and why.

The history of Earth has been a very long and tragic one for the most part, but without the realizations We have now of what Our own gaps were doing to oppose Us, We could not do any better. Those of you who are not yet willing to take responsibility for what you have done in your own gaps should not read this book, either. It is not right time for you. You need more movement in your emotions and more readiness to look at your own perpetration until you find that the Search for True Understanding and Balance is not necessarily holding onto or defending your own point of view. As long as you feel you must hold onto certain points of view and have not been able to accept and feel the fear of what changing them or being wrong might mean, you may be preferring to think you already have True Understanding and Balance.

All of life, for the Four Parts of God, has been a search for True Understanding and Balance, but the past lives I am going to go into here are particularly exemplary of this search in that they are lives that have impacted many people. You will have to go into these lives yourselves to find your own participation there which will relate very closely to your own Original Cause positioning, especially in the gaps We are looking at now for healing. If you were not there, you can still learn from what happened there.

These lives are not easy to read and understand in the ways they need to be read and understood. You are probably going to have to struggle with the painful parts, not even knowing why you have to read them at first, because they are not the usual superficial presentations of these time periods that give Us no new information and which have often obscured or deliberately omitted important points according to what points of view were going to be preserved or put forward as all there was there. These are not pleasant pictures of historical figures. They did not even live long, because they could not handle the struggles they found themselves to be trapped in. It is not possible to have it go on like this anymore; feeling is that healing must take place, and that it must take place now. If you feel this way, you need also to be ready to go into the depths of your own being, and ask for My Loving Light to be present there, for it is within My Loving Light that you will find your own True Understanding and Balance.

THE MOTHER AND LOST WILL OF HEART

As with everything I have given in these books, more happened than can be put in these linear pages. Sometimes, I have passed through things more than once in order to give more information. Emotional movement is so important for your own healing to help you know more of what you need to know, not only of what the Main Body of essence has experienced, but also what you, yourself, have experienced from your positioning relative to Them. The Mother is going to be the One talking in these first two sections, but it is My Loving Light that has given Her the words. Without that, She still would have no words, but She has agreement with the words I have given Her here.

I originally felt Heart as an intense longing for relationship welling up through whatever parts of Me I was aware of then. I felt like this longing was rising up and even out of Me in places, especially through what I would later come to feel was My Heart area, but then, I did not know it because form was not yet formed the way it is now. It was a pleasant feeling; full and good, welcome, soft and warm, like flower petals opening after such a long time of no feelings of expansion, but it ached for fulfillment. It was as though there was a swelling in My breast like a heart aching for love in the burst of Springtime. I experienced these feelings as part of Me, and strongly felt that this light I was beginning to perceive after so long a time in the dark void was going to bring Us that wanted fulfillment.

The feeling of wanting this light was so strong, I felt I was overflowing with desire for it. I had such feelings of release, relief, excitement, joy and fulfillment at last, that finally there was something I could relate to and have for companionship! I wasn't alone! I had feelings of such longing and hope for this light! I had, for such a long time, been so outwardly focused with My desire for something to come to Me so I wouldn't be alone. Sometime during this time, My Heart had begun to arise from this desire, and had been wanting to let Me know I wasn't alone there, but felt unsuccessful in Her attempts. I didn't experience Heart as a companion there. I experienced these feelings as a persistent desire in Myself for relationship. Without My realizing it, parts of My Heart had begun to feel insulted, ignored, overlooked, undervalued and neglected there, and wanted Me to pay more attention to It. This is how there came to be anger in Heart that It was not enough and was unappreciated by the Mother. This is also how self-love was damaged there by fear that this was narcissistic, and how My denied fears that this was all there was, and that I should be feeling this was all I needed, took form as some of the Mother Warriors and as Lesbians.

At the time, there was nothing I noticed more than these beginning perceptions of light. Some parts of My Heart began to feel that I was fixated on this light, or male, as Our salvation when these parts didn't feel that it was. They wanted Us to be Our own light, which We were, more than I knew. Soon after that, I began to notice that this light I'd been trying to draw did not appear to be coming into the area where I was. Suddenly, I realized that it hadn't occurred to Me that this light wouldn't share My exuberance. I did not understand its reluctance. I sank, feeling unwanted, rejected, confused, crushed, ashamed, embarrassed, delusional, frightened and even terrified about Myself and this light. I had lost My confidence, My momentum, My direction, My purpose. This light could not be desiring Me the way I wanted it, I felt, or it would notice Me more and respond to Me in some way.

I had no awareness of relativity other than My feelings and My perception of the light. I didn't know if I was moving toward this light or not. I did not know how to move. My feeling of movement was a feeling of wanting to draw closer together. I experienced movement as a feeling taking place within Me that I could not hold back this growing feeling of desire, longing and excitation, but I had also begun to fear that I actually could burst or be ripped apart, somehow, by this increase in the feelings of expansion within Me. I didn't notice that I was also, now, hanging back in fear that this light didn't like Me.

What I had hoped was a newfound happiness had begun to feel more unpleasant than I had wanted to acknowledge. What wanted to burst forth, that I would now call Heart Spirits, began to feel in resistance to how I now felt. Some of It wanted Me to turn within and give up My fixation on light. Another part was still urging Me with "Let's go for the light." I felt an edge of anger toward Me there. After so long of longing, I was feeling a distrust and caution, or reluctance. I no longer felt I knew what to do. I was quite awash in fears that I did not know how I felt, how I felt about this light or how it felt about Me, if it wanted Me or even if I wanted it anymore. As I felt that what had wanted to burst forth from Me was still wanting to go toward this light, I felt, more and more, as though I was sinking in the fear that there was no light for Me, and for some reason, I could not be reassured.

As much as I had wanted relief from the pressure I had been feeling there, I also wanted to hold this excited essence back. I had a feeling of dread that maybe I didn't know what We were in for. I didn't want part of Me to leave Me this way. Something I had barely begun to experience as a part of Me seemed to want to leave Me before I could know anything more about it, and in its determination to leave Me, I became lost Will. I feared it was exasperated with Me because I was in fear of what all of these uncomfortable feelings were going to mean for My chances with this light. I feared that what wanted to, and had actually begun to go forth from Me, just did not like Me and was not sharing with Me what it knew. "Find Your Own way, then!" this part of Me seemed to say. I felt left there with all the feelings it didn't want. I didn't want them either, and now, I had the additional fear that these feelings were all I was. After all, I had had them before, and it now felt like many times. What if these other feelings of excitement, hope and adventure were only a fleeting illusion as it now seemed I had also had so many times before.

Heart did not feel integrated with the rest of Me in these places, and as I found out later, even felt rejected and diminished by Me, as did I by Heart there. I had fears swamping Me, as though they were backwashing from My Heart area, and as big as these feelings were getting, I was not able to pay attention to anything else. There were suddenly so many feelings moving in Me now, all feeling as though they were trying to grab My attention at once. Many of them were feelings I had not felt ready to have so quickly right there with the feelings of My Heart swelling like love bursting forth in the Springtime. I felt overcome by these uncomfortable feelings. I felt pulled into an internal struggle.

Terror was there around no response from this light. There were feelings of such a heartache and longing that had been there for so long that it seemed to Me they had died, or nearly died, in unrequited agony, and as they stirred again now, it was almost immediate heartbreak the moment this light did not seem to be responding to Me the way I wanted it to. I felt unwanted, and now abandoned. Bitterness became judgments that accompanied these emotions. "Nothing wants Me," and "There's nothing that feels good to Me after all," are two of them. Excitation had stirred this essence back to life with what now felt like false promises and hope that there was, at last, something there for Us, but, "it was for nothing, because nothing good was going to come Our way after all."

Since it seemed that I did not yet know this light, if I had had words, they most likely would have said, "Perhaps this light is only a projection of My desperation for companionship. Maybe this light is only My imagination as I feared it had been in the past. Maybe this light has better things to do than sink into the mire of these feelings that felt so dense to Me."

I feared that My Heart was only chasing fantasies or dreams, and it was My fault. However, underneath and pushed away because I did not feel I wanted this to be a part of My feelings there, I felt resentment and even fury toward this light for its lack of responsiveness to Me. In this place, I imprinted the light as cold, uncaring, unfeeling, unresponsive and even cruel in its lack of response to Me, and if this light wasn't real, then I hated Myself even more than I already did.

I did not want to let Myself notice this for a long time, though. How could I resent, even hate and want to mutilate and punish, something I longed for so much? I did not understand how these feelings could co-exist, but I had these feelings, nonetheless, and rather immediately felt that I hated these feelings and did not want to let them have any voice with Me. I judged them to be irrational and unloving feelings.

As I wallowed and felt awash, and as though I was sinking and drowning in these feelings, the light was beginning to sparkle like a party going on somewhere else. "Without the old hag" voiced itself in Me somewhere. Perceiving that, I felt all the worse because, admit it or not, I did want to be a part of it. I hoped whatever had left Me hadn't already given this light unpleasant impressions of Me, but I was afraid that It had. If It had, what room was there going to be for Me? Why would this light ever come to Me if all I had for it were these feelings? I feared that if I tried to go to it, I would be rejected. "Who would want Me?" was My feeling there.

It seemed like such an interminably long time I had had these feelings of longing that I felt too old to go to a party now, anyway. I decided to stay home in My fear and let My excitation go forward. I sank down into depression and did not realize I had a rage smoldering there. Later, I realized that this rage had wanted Me to listen to it, but I didn't want to. In all of this, I still wanted the light to want Me and tell Me that no matter how I felt, it was alright. I was not very direct about it, though. I did not know how to make that known without feeling like I was inviting Myself to the party to then not feel able to trust that I was wanted there.

I was hoping this light would notice how I felt and make Me feel invited instead of feeling like I had to invite Myself when I was not sure if I was wanted or not. I was not even sure if I wanted Myself, or not, the way I was there, but I was hoping for something to help My feelings go through a change. I hoped this could happen if the light would come all of the way into Me and accept all of Me, instead of parts leaving Me. It felt like so much wanted to leave, and should, because I was a sinking ship. The bitterness there also pushed out some essence that was reluctant to go, but more reluctant from guilt, I feared, than anything else. It felt to Me like, one way or another, nearly everything wanted to leave the unwelcome feelings behind that I feared were Me.

In My fear of how to present to the light, I had had many faces appear in Me. These many changing faces were as though there was a fast flipping through of many female photograph portfolios and a trying on of identities the way some women go through clothing changes trying to decide what to wear when they're getting ready to go out. It felt like attempts to make the right presentation to this light in the form of, "To love Me, do you need Me to look like this, like this, like this, like this, like this?"

When essence had first begun to stir in My Heart area, I had seen many faces there also, as if They were getting ready to unfold as separate, but there seemed to be a lot of confusion around the progression of it and, also, rivalry. The more I couldn't help but look at the beauty and charm in these faces, the more I felt inadequate and the less I felt I could go anywhere with Them. I was in awe of so many of these faces, but also, in Myself and, now, in My Heart area, I also saw many faces whose look and feel I didn't particularly like. Some even winced away from Me, and some brought up feelings of shame. Some of them moved away whenever I tried to look at them, but some of them stayed closer to Me. I feared that whatever was pretty was not Me, that these faces I didn't particularly like were My faces, that this was all there was to Me and that I was not pretty. I imprinted there that I was ugly and that only pretty gets love, acceptance and attention. I feared that My earlier dreams had been too self-aggrandizing. I did not realize these were all pictures of My fears.

It had been one of My dreams to have a bouquet of the many faces of My love to present to the light if it came to Me, but the more I saw Them doing what I perceived as posturing and posing and looking good, the less I felt I could go anywhere with Them. My dream felt swept away from Me, not only by Their great exuberance, but also by what felt like a false self-confidence amongst them. I was unsure of what I looked like, so I did not know what was a true reflection, but I did not like the reflection of My uncomfortableness there. I felt way too self-conscious to act on My dream now.

It now seems to Me that the feelings I did not like there were a mingling of survival terror and other feelings that were underlying this exuberance to go forth with competition, anger and desperation lest this opportunity be lost. At the time, I only let Myself notice that they seemed to want to be desired the most and noticed first, which gave these faces the feeling of pushiness I did not like having there. It didn't feel good to Me, but I did not understand what I was projecting into My Heart. I thought that these must be their faces to have and not Mine. I pushed away any feelings I had that they could all be in competition with Me and each other because the unpleasantness of feeling that frightened Me that it would destroy the fragile bonds of love that I so wanted to grow. I imprinted My feelings there as judgmental, cold, unkind and unloving. I really wanted to be loved no matter what, but, at the time, I wasn't able to love Myself no matter what.

ANOTHER FRIGHTENING LOST WILL FRAGMENTATION

As essence from Me had begun to go forward, it began to seem that, at last, the light was responding; but as something began to come forth from the light, whatever it was, it was suddenly pushed right past what was going forth from Me and came falling into Me feeling very confused. I, too, was startled, frightened and confused, although I was also glad to have anything come My way. Even though We both had the feeling that this was not how We had wanted it to be. I also felt this essence might be a gift. This essence, however, felt to Me like He was not glad to be where He was. We were both imprinted heavily by this experience.

He felt frightened about Himself, as though maybe He was wrong to have gone forth, or was not wanted, or was not wanted as a part of the light that had pushed Him here. He conveyed that He had felt confident that He was loving, but this experience had imprinted confusion about love and self-sacrifice. He had felt He knew how it should have gone there, and now was fearing He wasn't really loving and was trying to make too much of Himself by trying to take a position that wasn't really His to take. He began to fear He didn't really belong anywhere as He didn't feel like My mate. He felt very young to Me, and both of Us had feelings of wanting to bond in a way other than mate, but here We were without anyone else around. The concept of fatherless child arose in Me here, and male Heart's rage felt huge toward the father He felt had done this to Him.

His feeling was that He had wanted the light where He already was to bond with Me, and then He would take what was coming forth from Me, later recognized as Daughter, into His arms and begin a relationship with Her. He felt He had been cruelly separated out of where He had been and shoved down and out as though His romantic desire was not wanted, right or welcome there. When My response was mixed, He feared again that His input was not welcome. He also felt that since He had emerged downward from My lower area where He had fallen into Me, that He had been shoved toward sex too soon as though that was all that was wanted there. He felt there were angry voices still on Him saying, "This is what You were urging toward, this is what You wanted, here it is, so go for it!

He felt misunderstood, maybe deliberately misunderstood. He was angry and frightened about what all of this meant and utterly heartbroken and afraid the love He wanted to find had been stolen from Him, and He could never have it now. We felt desolate and couldn't help noticing that the light wasn't coming toward either of Us. I could not seem to comfort Him and feared He might be taking My attempts as a sexual advance. I feared again that My dream of love could not be realized.

Meanwhile, We were growing increasingly terrified of the compression We were in and desperately wanted help. The longer this went on and nothing returned to Us from the other side, the more We felt washed back in the wake of something that had abandoned Us. The feeling was one of a life boat having filled up with the people it wanted and then moving away in order to ignore what was going to happen to the others.

As this went on, I could feel this part of Heart hardening Himself against the circumstances He found Himself in. Oh, how I wished I could comfort Him, change this or stop feeling it too, but I didn't know how, and pretty soon, I began to feel like I didn't know how to communicate with Him. I so wanted to communicate how I felt to Him, but He didn't seem to want to receive it because it caused Him to feel it again too, and neither of Us knew how feeling it could make it any better. This part of Heart has not felt able to find His right place as a part of Heart since He felt pushed out of the place He was headed for.

The feeling of expansion in My Heart area and the feeling of it wanting to go forth has remained as My original impression of how Heart was going to emerge, but I had wanted it to be more gentle than it had felt. When exuberance took over, I wouldn't have minded except for the edge on it that felt angry, pushy and competitive for position, leaving some out entirely as though it had turned its back on them. I didn't know, at the time, how much of this was fear based. I didn't know how or why My original dream of a courtship got swept away, either. Neither the part of Heart that had come to Me, nor I, knew, then, why Our original desires had been so thwarted or what was wrong with them, but something did not feel good or right to Us about what happened there. We began living with bitterness, regret and remorse, and have had a difficult time finding peace about what happened there and the form this took.

There were times when We tried to hold onto Each Other, but could not do it very well. It seemed that Our awareness lapsed at times, and at those times We would sometimes let go of Each Other and become lost from One Another. This was extremely terrifying to Me. It felt to Me that any more desperate loneliness in the darkness was more than I could, or wanted to have to handle, and I didn't want to lose Heart. Sometimes, it seemed like a long time before We vibrated at all again, yet, either Our fear of death or Our desire to try to live, for what reasons We did not even really know anymore, would draw Us together again.

Fearing the crushing presence of compression, We were trying to fight to survive however We could and, not knowing how to do that, were trying anything that might make Us feel better. At times, We felt We needed to find a way to make noise, some of it loud noise, and lots of it, but when We tried to make sounds, We would feel unreal, hate ourselves for the way We sounded there and feel that We had to shut Ourselves down. We could only express little pieces of the noise We wanted to make before something would make Us feel confirmed in this, instead of helping Us to feel encouraged there. Not only did We hate our situation, We hated Ourselves and hated Ourselves for hating Ourselves and did not know why. We didn't understand what the problem was here or feel able to just accept Ourselves and let it happen, any more than We could accept it that We were going out of existence in compression and terror.

We felt We had to do whatever We could to try to feel better in secret, but did not know why, since there seemed to be no one else around. Even so, We still feared that what We were doing was somehow wrong and shameful. We did not really feel like mates. We felt like Mother and Son, but even when We just wanted to comfort Each Other, We were still afraid without knowing why. It didn't make sense when those who had left Us weren't showing Us anything to make Us feel they had any interest in ever coming back to Us, yet, We still felt fear of displeasing them as though Our beings were already committed to them. We even had fear of hurting them and fear they were going to strike at Us for hurting them. We tried to push those feelings aside in favor of what seemed to make more sense, which was that they weren't coming back, and so, We only had Each Other; but the feelings persisted anyway, and now, there was a voice We were hearing that said things like, "You are only feeling sorry for Yourselves! Get over it!"

This part of Heart and I would lie together for long periods of time, sinking down and down into these feelings, the intensity of which was overwhelming to Us as physical sensations, also. The pain felt unbearable, and for long periods of time, I could not even make a sound because it took so much just to stay conscious in all of this. I felt guilty as though I was accusing Him wrongly, but I began to fear Heart was going to kill Me to get rid of these feelings. I hardly dared communicate this to Him when He seemed to be My only companion, but found Myself sending pleading feelings to Him, that if We'd had words, would have said, "Please! Don't hurt Me! Don't push Me farther down into terror! Don't abandon Me! Please don't kill Me!"

These feelings were extremely terrifying to Me, and from them, images had begun to arise of Heart doing terrible things to Me. This must have meant some light was coming there, but this was not the kind of light I wanted to have. Heart was trying to reach Me in those deep places, hoping that if He touched Me in the right way there, that it would bring forth the healing that had, so far, seemed to elude Us. I began to feel that I needed loving touch to be slow and deep because of My pain and damage, but I wasn't really sure of what I needed. I had hope that Heart knew or would discover it, but as My feelings of dark, compression terror went on, it seemed that He didn't know or couldn't give

Me what I needed. At times, Heart got so frustrated that He felt enraged and did have feelings of wanting to beat Me up and get rid of Me. When I felt this, I would also feel hatred for Myself, but fear would cause Me to beg Him not to do it, and not to leave Me alone.

In Our lack of any help understanding Our predicament, We sometimes sank deeply enough into Ourselves that We fell into a silence that seemed to bring some relief by feeling nothing, but I feared I was close to death then and would startle Myself into suffering again as somehow preferable to death. We experienced dark compression for so long there before We began to experience any light, and Heart and I felt so impacted by this experience, that We didn't know how anyone else could relate to Us now, especially since We had had experiences there in the darkness that had felt sexual, either directly or indirectly, and We felt full of shame and a sense of wanting to hide what We had done.

As much as We were frightened by and ashamed of Our approach there and of how We had not found another way other than to go through such terrible feelings to find even a small place of pleasure in Ourselves, We began also to fear that We were terribly twisted and sick to have to sink down into so much compression, terror and pain to find these feelings. It seemed that We couldn't even dare to acknowledge this to Ourselves or Each Other. We buried most of our self-loathing there along with much of Our sexual fear and shame.

This was how this part of Heart and I initially got into sex together. We didn't realize, at first, that it was sex, because We were just trying to reach into Each Other as deeply as possible. Heart felt that He understood Me here, and that I understood Him. I wanted Him to touch Me deeply and help Me feel better, and I felt like He wanted that from Me, but while I wanted constant touch, He seemed to only want it at times. There was something there that was difficult for either of Us to face. The feeling that We were not mates was amplifying Our feelings that Our relationship was wrong. This was amplifying Heart's feelings of inadequacy and no right place and My feelings of rejection, self-hatred and fear that I could not make Myself feel the way I was wanted to feel.

I felt so inadequate I could hardly dare to let Myself feel it, and I feared Heart felt that way also. We felt so unwanted and inadequate. I was trying to make Myself accept what was happening, as though it was supposed to be or was right somehow. Heart was trying so hard to be the man and the father He thought He needed to be there that it was heartbreaking to Me to experience Him trying to be father when He so badly needed a father for Himself.

We didn't know, in the beginning here, how to attract, draw or generate Loving Light. Nonetheless, what We were doing there was helping Us to raise Our vibration more than either of Us realized, but then We began to feel attacked by zots of light. They were small at first, but grew bigger as time went on, until it seemed like nothing noticed Us as long as We were unconscious or nearly dead, but when We started to feel good and feel the least little bit like We might recover, something seemed to notice Us that felt to Us like it wanted to push Us back down.

It started with little zots of light in Heart's back that I did not know about at first, and when I did, I had feelings of wanting to protect Him there. I had feelings of wanting the light to be softer than this because this hurt, but not having consciously received it before, I did not know how light was supposed to feel, or needed to feel, coming in. Sometimes Heart would get so enraged after receiving this light that He would start punishing Me as though it was all My fault that it was happening the way it was. It was only My rage that did not fear He was right, and the rest of Me imprinted that I did not know how to receive anything.

The feelings I was having sexually there began co-existing with the punishment. I did not like the punishment aspect at all and communicated that to Heart every time, but sometimes, it did startle and distract Me and took My attention off of My resistance to orgasm, but then, after orgasm, I would feel shame. Heart would convey to Me that He did not know what made Him do it. It seemed to

Me that the little healing We had done was easily reversed by these attacks. I was so near to being a corpse there that I feared He was going to do Me enough additional damage that I really would be a corpse. I could not find much reason to protest becoming a corpse except for some survival drive that did not make sense in My situation. I saw it more as fear of the compression and the feeling of not wanting to abandon Heart there, even though I often had feelings that He would somehow be better off without Me and would prefer it even if He missed Me at first.

The zots of light continued, and they continued to make Heart feel fits of rage toward Me. Then, Heart let Me know that these zots of light were giving Him messages to kill Me, or at least abandon Me, saying I was the reason He wasn't getting to have the life He wanted to have. I feared He felt these zots were right. The longer this went on, the bigger and more frequent these zots of light became, as though, if He did not comply with them, they were going to hurt Him until He did.

I was deeply terrified. I did not know how aligned He really was with these messages and images because He would not communicate with Me about them. I cried in Heart's arms, but the feelings were way more than I dared express there. I feared for the struggle Heart was having, and that He could turn on Me at any point when this light hit Him. It was bad enough to feel what We already felt there, but the next rage message, or zot of light, would usually say exactly what We had been fearing without having any words for it. The zots of light would say things to Him like this, "She's not getting any better, so put Her out of Her misery and go have a life! She's not able to live because She can't live. She won't let anyone help Her. She can't be helped. She's the reason You can't have the life You want. Get rid of Her!"

He would say it to Me like this, "You're not getting any better. You won't let Me help You! I should just put You out of Your misery and leave. You're the reason I don't have any life. You won't let Me have any life."

There were other messages like this, "You have let Yourselves get too damaged to live like this anymore, but You are too terrified to surrender to death." He would give it to Me as, "You are too damaged to live, but You're too afraid of death to die."

Next message, "You can't be free, because You won't let go and let it happen the way it is meant to."

These messages gave Us the feeling that We were being watched and listened to somehow, but We did not like the way it felt. It felt like that light knew everything about Us, but for some reason would not help Us, or at least, not Me. I began to be fatalistically bitter, even self-destructive and acted like I didn't care what happened to Me. Perhaps, I wanted death to overtake Me when I didn't know it was going to happen. Smoldering rage was very stirred up over this and was telling Me not to listen to anything from this light or even feel like I needed it. It didn't seem to have any sympathy for Me, either. Was it not feeling the compression terror I was in? My heart was hardening here, though, and I didn't know how much.

Next message, "Let go of everything You desire and accept however it is."

We tried to apply this, but We didn't know how and couldn't, and at the bottom of it, We didn't feel, or at least I didn't feel, that this was right.

I felt Heart being drawn away from Me by these zots of light, even though He denied it, and I feared that I was not wanted to live and was not supposed to live. Heart began to leave Me sometimes then. I felt like He was somehow able to roam around, although I did not know where He really went or what He really did. I hoped and feared that He was looking for the voice, or whatever was attacking Us, but I was afraid to ask or complain. At least He did return, and at least He was there with Me at times, and no matter how much I told Myself I would not ask or complain, I often did. I felt that Heart was drawn more and more away from Me, and although He never completely abandoned Me, I feared Him when He returned enraged, and I feared His rage could return at any moment when He came back feeling hopeless. Sometimes, He said He hated His rage and that He only wanted to love Me. The more He said it, the more it felt like He was trying to convince Himself, but Heart knew what He was struggling with here better than I did.

Both the rage that was zotting Heart and My rage felt to Us like it was scornful of Us. The fragmentation here has been a formidable bunch of children to face; especially when they claimed they were nobody's child and didn't need "nuttin'" or nobody," except when they wanted to blame Us or insist that We had to do something for them. Whether it was all fragmentation or not, the lost Will of Heart that was with Me there was the parental part, without knowing it, of all of these other pieces of the denied and lost Will of Heart that need healing now.

These lost pieces of Heart postured as though they didn't mind being displaced and had chosen to remove themselves from the horrible, dysfunctional scene that We had going on because there "ain't no parents or home anyway," but then it didn't look to Me like they had any place at all because I didn't know there was a "scene" going on "out there" in the darkness that they were joining into. I just knew I was becoming more frightened of this rage turning on Heart when He went roaming alone, or turning on Me when I was alone. I didn't want to mention this to Heart for fear He was going to say that nothing He ever did was good enough for Me, that I never liked it and that I was never satisfied, which He did say, in so many words, many times.

Heart also had times when He would cry piteously like a child who was trapped in a nightmare, and who certainly had no father anymore, and no mother, either, for that matter; certainly not one who could help Him get out of His horrors. I cried, too, then and felt terribly unprepared to be a mother and horribly inadequate. I tried to hide My fears more and do whatever I could, because I did not want Him to have to feel this way. When I hid My fears more, it seemed that He hid His more, too.

We managed to present as a little more cheerful at times, then. A little cheerfulness, presentation or not, seemed better, but it left Us alone in Our own fears and terrors, and the more We tried to ignore them, the more it left these emotions alone, isolated, without help, hated by everyone, and now, Us, too. We told Ourselves We were getting better, but the more We tried not to go into these feelings, especially bitter hopelessness and terror, the more We noticed a fear that We could be consumed by them, and the less We felt able to be there for Ourselves or for Each Other.

Some of these unwanted feelings had been taking form as trapped and defenseless babies and very small children with no one to guide or help them, no love for them, no life for them, no way out, no one coming to rescue them, take care of them, comfort them or help them in any way; only attack them, and they had no way to cry out or even speak of their plight to anyone who would receive them. They had the fear and terror that they deserved it as the cause of unhappiness and everything that went wrong. They could not come up in vibration; they could not grow up. They could only suffer and die as unwanted little infants and children lost in the horrors of the darkness, torture and terror We had felt Ourselves to be in there.

The only parents they have had have been the personified hatred We had for what they represented to Us there, and the personified hatred We feared the zots of light had for Us that confused Us instead of helping Us and amplified Our feelings of being twisted and evil. These children have been punished, tortured and gotten rid in all the gruesome and grisly ways that had arisen in Us from Our fears about Ourselves, and the reflection was so frightening to Us that We feared to look at it. This fragmentation has felt scorned by Us, isolated and trapped with no way out and has been born into this over and over, hardening itself in defensive anger, resentment and hatred. This fragmentation must be helped now by healing Our own self-hatred.

ANOTHER LOOK AT THE PURPLE GAP

After what seemed like an interminably long time of being trapped in darkness, compression and pain, the light that had seemed so lost from Us finally began to seem as though it might be coming closer to Us again. I hoped this meant it wanted to include Us now. Soon, it was looking even bigger and brighter than before, unless I didn't remember it clearly. I feared, then, that maybe it was only looking like it was coming closer because it was getting so much bigger and brighter.

I began to feel a tingling excitation from its presence, or from the awareness of its presence. I became aware of things I had not been aware of for a long time. I felt, then, that I must have had a gap in My awareness of Myself since I had not noticed the feeling of this light before or a gradual increase in its presence. It felt sudden to Me and like a sudden awakening. I felt fear about Myself again. I wanted to turn toward Heart to see if He was experiencing the same thing, when I suddenly noticed He was not there. Nor, could I feel Him anywhere nearby.

I had so many feelings in response to Heart's absence that I could not even begin to understand them or sort them out. I felt frozen in a horrible feeling inside Myself, watching this light either grow bigger or seem to come closer without feeling able to perceive which. At first, I was aware of only white light, but as I looked more closely, I saw many pastel colors, all dancing. I was entranced by them all, and excited, as though I was receiving a reward for all My suffering. I also did not feel content just to see them. I wanted to feel them, be amongst them and experience them, but I feared rejection so much I was afraid to even try to move toward it and again judged Myself very heavily without knowing I was doing it. I felt frozen in self-hatred, looking at this light and feeling unable to move toward it. It was as though something other than Me was preventing Me.

There was, however, one color I began to feel particularly drawn to go toward first. I felt that Heart had somehow gone there. It was a Purple color, not very bright, but Purple, nonetheless. I began to feel compelled, even urgent to go there, as if it was hope springing forth in Me again, but I did not trust it. I felt dread, fear and reluctance and judged all of My feelings there. I was awash in an anguish and hated Myself for how I was feeling.

I wanted to go to this Purple light, but fear was holding Me back from making any move at all. It was like having a fight with Myself between hope and fear that was giving Me a push-pull, go-stay polarization. As soon as one part wanted to go, another part wanted to stay, and vice versa. I couldn't get an alignment in Myself and didn't know why. Hope seemed to be the side to go with, but fear felt stronger, and the more I hoped, the more I feared.

Right about then, I began to have quite a distinct feeling that Heart had found Purple. I wanted to find Heart, but felt hesitant. I didn't feel it was a message to come there, only that He was there and was going to stay there for a while and see what was happening. I was glad to hear from Heart at all, but also disappointed that the message felt mixed. It was a feeling of come if you want to, but not a feeling that He wanted Me to come. It felt to Me as though He did not want to let Me know anything or really have Me come there. Purple felt that way to Me entirely. Maybe Heart was insecure there. I didn't feel like My presence would not do anything to steady Him there.

I let fear hold Me back then. Waiting for an invitation to come to Purple, I began to grow more and more impatient and restless that He was not calling Me to join Him there. I had also been trying to draw this light to Me, but it did not seem to be coming to Me. I feared that I was delusional and/ or not wanted, but still, I felt I had to go to that Purple light. As My attention became more focused there, I began to hear sounds as though there was noisy sex going on, and some of it sounded very angry to Me. Feelings of shame and fear welled up in Me. I wanted to go and see what Heart was doing in Purple, but I felt very afraid of what I might see and feel there.

There were also sounds coming from Purple as if music was starting to happen. I was intensely tuned, with all the desire I had there, toward hearing these sounds. It seemed to Me that I could even smell Purple wafting down through the ethers, like incense from a party. I felt intoxicated by the desire to go and felt so drawn to go there that I felt I could not let My fear hold Me back anymore. I exhorted Myself to get over My fear, and in so doing lost all sense of Myself except for My desire to go to Purple. Even though great fear had been holding Me back, rather suddenly, I seemed to burst forth and set out for Purple.

I felt driven by a feeling that I had to know what was happening there, invitation or no invitation. All the way there, I met resistance that seemed to be telling Me not to go. I would hesitate for a while and try to stay where I was, but then, I would feel I had to resume My journey to Purple. Even though I feared this could not be trusted and was only My own hopes and desires to go, I felt compelled to go to Purple. .

I traveled a long way, it seemed, but it could have been not much in terms of outer movement or even nowhere at all really, except a vibrational change. It was all at the feeling level for Me, but I experienced it as very difficult to get to where Purple was coalescing. There seemed to be a lot in the way that was protesting and resisting My desire there, and the go-don't-go continued within Me, too. Even though I tried to ignore it, I felt intensely afraid of meeting rejection, or worse. When I finally found Purple, I felt intensely agitated, and in My longing for Heart, shame could not admit that I might also have felt sexually excited.

I had only reached what I felt within Myself to be the womb in Purple, when I was shocked to feel clamped down on and held there as though trapped. I could not move upward, or even move at all. I felt trapped in suffocating, lonely, and now, dark compression again. I began to struggle the way Heart and I had done in the darkness and felt clamped down on even more. I felt desperate to express emotions in response to what I felt happening there, but

I couldn't. Feeling frantic, I quickly became desperately panicky. Telling fear it had been right all along, I fervently wished I had never left home to feel stopped and compressed all over again. Horrible as it had been where I was, I seemed to forget that in My frantic panic of feeling trapped and unable to alleviate My compression terror. Getting back out of there became all I wanted.

I could see the face of a woman, a face that was many faces, above Me there, looking tantalizingly beautiful and showing no expression of caring or noticing that I was there or of what I was feeling. I felt disoriented then. What were these faces? Who did I feel I was that I could have any business at all trying to be there? I felt self-loathing then, but I did not like another presence in the place I wanted to have, which was the loving presence with the male energy, and that became all I could think of in the midst of the terror and terrible feelings of entrapment I was experiencing.

The light had felt so tantalizingly close, and now, I was not able to reach it or make My presence known in any way. I felt My presence not being made welcome there. I felt trapped, compressed, silenced, ignored and hidden, as though My presence was not even going to be acknowledged there. The terror of feeling that whatever had clamped down on Me was going to suffocate Me to death without even caring or acknowledging I was there, felt more than overwhelming to Me. Frantically panicky, I tried to deny this in favor of something more pleasant, but it seemed to Me that I felt a message of, "one woman here, and You are not the one."

I so badly wanted to get back out of there and go hide somewhere with My fears and shame. I was desperate to escape My entrapment there and don't know how I actually did it. Anger must have helped Me wrench Myself back out of there, but it didn't feel like I got out with all of Myself. I tried to reach back for Myself, and the female presence in Purple must have felt it, because I was quickly clamped down on. Still, I continued to try reaching back for the rest of Myself, but felt unable to recover those parts of Myself. I was confused. Did this part of Me not want to leave Purple, was the female presence in Purple doing this to Me, was Heart somehow pushing Me back and down? What was happening to Me?

That part of Me could want to stay in a place that felt this terrible sickened Me with fear that I was so needy I would stay there no matter how it felt. I decided these parts of Me might be too suffocated to respond to Me, but when I again tried to reach back for them, she clamped down on Me again. I feared she was trying to trap more of Me. A fear arose in Me, suddenly, that she was trying to make Me into her child. I felt trapped and split. I did not want to be her child, but I had not been able to recover those parts of Myself. I feared being uninvited, unwanted and unwelcome there, but I also could not leave those parts there. Why, I no longer knew. It was as if I couldn't keep a hold of Myself there.

Each time I tried to go back for those parts of Myself, I felt more frightened and hopeless about the situation. More and more, it felt like part of Me was trapped, unable to move, in another woman who was in the place I most wanted to have and that I could do nothing about it. It felt like she was heartlessly stealing something from Me that she was going to use, and I was not going to like the results. The something arising in Me that didn't want to let go of the place I had in Purple, even if it was lowly, is how part of Me became a midwife and nursemaid in Purple.

Each time I tried to reach back for the trapped parts of Myself, I also saw a fuller vision of her than I had seen before. She was looking more and more vividly formed in the ways I wanted to be formed there, like a beautiful, purple flower with gorgeous faces. She smelled intoxicatingly exquisite and looked soft, feminine and luscious. She looked like everything I wanted to be and felt I never could be; not anymore. She was gently undulating like flower petals in a gentle breeze. I could not stop looking at her beauty. I was transfixed, and so, she saw Me there. I must have been gaping with My mouth open because she kind of smiled as if to say, "What are you staring at?"

When she turned her gaze upon Me, I felt like the lowliest of maids who had gone into the queen's chamber unbidden and should not have stayed to get caught. I felt very awkward and ugly in her presence and felt that she did not want to have to notice Me or have Me there in any way. I felt ashamed not to have already accepted her clamping down as a clear message that I was not wanted there. She did not do anything to help Me with My feeling of confusion or misunderstanding, if it was one. Even so, I could not bring Myself to go back down.

She seemed so much more refined and reasonable, composed and articulate than I felt. I felt really guilty then, and feared I deserved to have her pushing down on Me as though I didn't know My place. I remembered then that I hadn't been invited. I felt I should go back down, but I didn't want to leave part of Myself there. She stared at Me as if she wanted to query Me. She startled Me by conveying to Me, "Oh, and why do You want to be here with me?"

"I'm looking for My man," I tried to convey to her, and then stammered, "My child, I mean."

She gazed at Me with a raised eyebrow sort of disdain that conveyed, "You won't find what You're looking for here. The only man here is my man."

"And My child?" I tried to convey.

"There is no child here," she replied.

I couldn't respond. I felt ashamed of Myself, then, and really frightened that I could have felt she had taken My man, but something felt persistent in Me that she had and that I was never going to get him back. To My surprise, she accused Me of trying to steal from her and pushed Me back rather quickly. Terrified that Heart was now in a place where I could never be, I felt Myself falling. I caught Myself as much as I could, but I was shaking uncontrollably and felt great anguish. With only a slight change of her expression, she conveyed to Me that she did not like it. She seemed so much more cool and composed than I felt in My swirl of emotions. Even though I was very uncomfortable in her presence, I felt that between missing Heart and feeling part of Myself imprisoned within her, I could not leave.

"Imprisoned?" she conveyed. "You are free to go."

I felt her current was really saying I wish You would go. I didn't go, though, because I needed to go with all of Me if I was going to go, and I could not communicate with her about this. When I tried to rise up with something to convey to her, I felt pushed back and down again by something conveying, "Go if you don't like it here. I told You already, You are free to go."

Lost in this, I felt Myself going numb from the feelings of suffocation I was experiencing there and felt I was going unconscious when I began to hear sounds that could be a male...familiar sounds, somehow. Suddenly, I was alert. The something in Me that didn't want another female presence in Purple in the position I wanted to have wanted Me to go forward and demand her place.

She turned her attention to this other presence, trying to capture his attention with her wiles. She was wafting her perfume in his direction. Her face looked demure and aloofly desirous of him, but it seemed to Me she felt uneasy now that she knew I was there. I felt excited as though this might be My man, but if he even seemed to start to move toward where I was, she moved with him, keeping herself between Us, trying to keep his attention on her and away from her womb area. She was acting like a girl on a date who wants to control where the male puts his hands. This male began to approach her sexually, and she began to resist like she didn't want to be touched sexually by him. She also seemed to be looking past him as if there was another man who wasn't going to like this at all. I desperately wanted to see who was there, and she continued to keep herself between Us.

It was a jealous rage that had begun to arise in Me, but jealous rage was not what I wanted to be feeling. I tried to hold it back. What was I doing there anyway! But jealous rage had another opinion. Jealous rage was strong and assertive and definitely did not want another presence in the place I wanted to have. Jealous rage felt blame that all My other feelings had been caused by lack of receptivity to

Me there, and, even though it seemed irrational, wanted to storm into Purple and demand to be included. I had wanted to be included in Purple, but now fear wasn't at all sure I was going to like it there after all.

There seemed to be no time for Me to feel into any of this, nor an ability to know what to do with it if I had. Jealous rage erupted with sniping energy sent toward this female presence in Purple beginning with, "You look pretty, but you feel terrible, like a heartless queen who won't let anyone else be here with you. You don't belong here. You went forward like the queen of it all, and left me with everything you didn't want; everything that didn't please him! Who is he anyway, and what are you doing here instead of me?"

She received this from behind, and without losing her composure, sent back a retort of, "You just want it to be your place. If it was your place, you'd be in it." She kept her attention on him.

Rage claimed not to be intimidated by this, but I was. I was cowering in fear of her and this rage. I didn't want this rage to ruin My chances. I wanted to bide our time and see what happened. I would not have wanted this to be the only message that went forth there, but I could not find Myself. I could feel her conveying, "I know better than you how to handle this. I have more experience. I was here first. How dare you come pushing your way up here now and start telling me how it is and what to do!"

I began to feel screaming streams of rage vibrations and didn't know who was sending them. The other male who was apparently there was being belittled with streams of, "You can't get it up. You're too much of a prude! You give her the promise, and then you never deliver and won't let me deliver, either! You're not going to hold me back anymore! I'm not going to take "no" for an answer anymore from you, either! If you think you're going to be able to have her, you can have her when I'm done with her! And you're never going to be able to satisfy her the way I'm going to! She's always going to be wanting me! Wishing for me! Fantasizing that I'll be the one to come and take her to the place she wants to go! You had your chance! You're impotent, and you know it! You just didn't want to let anyone else know! You backed me up until I couldn't do anything else but this, and now I'm the one she's always going to want!"

He also began to assault her with his rage. "You look at me with desirous eyes of allure and promise! I have come to you over and over, and then hear how you aren't sure if you want to go this way! Aren't sure if you want this position or that position! Aren't sure if you really called me! Didn't really call me! It's not really me you were calling! I'm not the one! Maybe if I was different, you would want me! Maybe if I was more the way you wanted me to be, you would want me!"

"But all that is true," she conveyed placidly and rather demurely.

This rang so familiar I cringed. I could feel his rage and cowered in dread of him. The more she denied desiring him, the more enraged this male was becoming. It felt like he was turning into a raging beast who could kill her or Us. Could this be Heart? I knew Heart in this place, and I was terrified of it. Oh, how I wished for the heart that felt loving to Me! Oh, how I wanted to get to her heart or find Heart! Then from him, "I've had enough! I'm not taking 'no' for an answer! You say you don't want me! I'm going to show you that you do want me! I'm going to take what you haven't given me! I'm going to make you scream and cry out for me and no one else. I am the only one for you!"

He began putting her in all sorts of sexual positions that she wasn't liking according to her body's reactions and the sounds she was making. "Let me in! Open to me!"

He was thrusting into her hard and deep and began growling at her, "I want to feel you want me! I want to hear you beg me to come into you the way I want to come into you! I don't want to hear any more excuses about 'not now, not this way, maybe that way, maybe later!' No claims you didn't call me or that it isn't really me you were calling! Don't tell me 'maybe if I was more the way you wanted me to be, you would want me!' I want to be wanted just the way I am! Give it to me and give it to me now! Let me in!"

She was streaming rage at him to stop and conveying that she didn't at all like what he was doing there. He studied her face, and then he seemed to dismiss her by conveying to her, "You like it! Stop acting so disgusted and admit you really want it!"

He flipped her over and went into her even more deeply from behind, touching her really deeply the way I wanted to be touched. I could feel it and was ashamed of My sexual feelings there. I couldn't look, but I could feel him starting to beat on her. He was streaming, "Give me the response I want here, or I'm going to make you wish you had! Give it up to me!"

He was getting more and more agitated and frantic. It felt like he wanted more intensity. It was becoming even more assaultive. He was slapping her and shaking her, and then, he put his hands around her neck and began to shake her and squeeze her neck as though he was going to strangle her. She was getting frantic and streaming hating energy at him, "Stop it! Stop it! You're hurting me! You're insisting it's you I was calling! I wasn't calling you! You're not who I want!" He was still shaking her and choking her and as he was having his orgasm, and dark things were rolling off of him doing even more terrible things. She felt hardened, angry and still insistent that she didn't want it.

It felt like Heart came to Me there. I felt even more confused. Then, there was more, "Stop it! Stop it!" from her which was disregarded with more blows, and then, "I hate you! You don't respect me! You don't care what happens to me! You don't love me! I hate you! I hate you! I hate you!"

I had the feeling that there was another male there, and if there was, why he didn't help her. Then, suddenly, from him, "I'll show you who hates who here! I hate you! I hate you both!"

He flipped her onto her backside and looked at her face. "Don't look at me with those eyes!" I felt him hit her in her beautiful face. "If you feel that way, you're not going to keep anything of me. I'm going to make it so you can't enjoy anyone else or keep anything of them in you, you thieving witch! You think you're going to have a child, but I'm going to make sure you can't have any children if you won't have mine." Then, indicating the other male I had thought was there, "He thinks there can still be children with him. We'll see what kind of children he has! Wimpy, like him!" I felt him beating on her womb as she was feeling more and more full of pain and sending out, "I hate you! I hate you!"

There was more assaultive energy streaming forth there, and feelings of grief. I felt him rip something out of her from where I'd been trapped. I felt him hold this part up. I felt him convey, "this is mine!" in what would have been growling sounds if sounds could have been made then in Purple. Why was he calling it his? I was afraid he was about to drop this piece into his large, open mouth and devour it. Then he seemed to change his mind, and he flung it down. Then, "You're disgusting! You're heartless! You don't care about me or how I feel! It's all about you! You're a miserable excuse for a woman and miserable sexually! Get out of my way! Both of you!"

As she saw him gathering himself to leave, I felt her convey to him in the equivalent of what would have been an under the breathe comment, "You're the one who's heartless and an insatiable beast! I'll hate you forever!"

When I later regained some consciousness, it felt like coming out of a severe surgical anesthesia or a very bad dream, except not a dream, because I had all the pain of it. Just as fear had said I would, I must have come crashing back from Purple. I felt completely alone and feared I had no way to have any help healing it now. I fell back into unconsciousness, and when I awoke, Heart was there with Me, but He did not seem to be conscious anymore. He seemed so small. I did not remember Him being so small. He seemed like an infant to Me now, and I did not feel like I knew how to help Him or what He would want Me to do for Him. He didn't seem to have any light.

It all felt so terrible I began to have weeping feelings and got the equivalent of tears all over Heart. Then, I was afraid I was making him cold, and I tried to hold Him close to Me. He gave no sign of life, and I could not stay conscious. After

I do not know how long, I was able to move a little. I held Heart close and kind of rocked Us, even though I felt Myself to be as though lying down and could not really move because My pain was so great. I could not get Us warm and could not help but weep and weep, fall into unconscious, come to, find Him still cold and weep more. I was not able to move through My grief there that life was never going to change for Us, and that Heart was never going to be conscious again, but I still hoped that He would. I felt like I couldn't live without Heart.

I kept trying to give Him nourishment in some way from My heart area; anything to get Him to have some life in him. After a lot of this, I began to feel some anger at Heart. I didn't want to feel angry at Heart, and the more I didn't convey this feeling to Heart, the more it felt like it was mounting up into hating Heart, hating what had happened and what was still happening and hating Myself for having these feelings. After a long time of this, I began to feel like I was going crazy in My hatred of it all and began screaming at Him, begging Him to come back to life somehow. As if this were going to help, I told Myself. I felt terrified that this was not loving of Me, but I could not stop Myself. I desperately wanted Heart to be there with Me and felt that wasn't loving of Me, either. How could I love Heart and want Him to come back to a life that was like this? 'Heart!' I screamed at Him finally, 'Get over it! You always expected Me to!'

A little while after that, Heart began to stir just the littlest bit. I really cried then. "I'm sorry! I'm sorry!" and held Him tighter and began to rock Him a little bit, sobbing all the while, "Please come back. Please come back," then more, "I'm sorry. I'm sorry. You don't have to come back if You don't want to; it's just that I need You so much! But, I'm selfish! You don't have to come back if You don't want to!"

Little by little, Heart began to come back to Me then. Even though I feared He was going to be angry at Me, too, I was feeling happiness about this and hoped that this love between Us would be enough to heal Us both.

PURPLE GAP'S INVOLVEMENT IN THE SPIRITUAL PROBLEMS ON EARTH

Having next to no understanding left Us with no real way to know what was really happening to Us there, but you need to understand it, so I cannot tell it the way I experienced it originally anymore. God is going to tell this from the perspective of the Spirit.

What happened in Original Cause was not just a linear series of events, and events are still not just linear. Our denials accompanied Us all along the way at varying distances and speeds depending on the force of Our denial.

What We thought We had left behind Us was getting more and more backed up, not only sexually backed up, but in every other way, too. In our gap, or subconsciously you might like to say now, this was what we wanted them to feel because we wanted to punish them. The idea of punishing them gave us more sexual turn-on than anything else, but we didn't let that be known. We held that in secret, sometimes splitting sexual titillation and punishment in our mind to the point of not letting ourselves notice this by pretending the two were not connected.

When they could not stand being backed up any more, their bodies would just seem to take over the situation. We saw that if they were miserable enough, they could be made to hate their emotionality and their physicality and not know why. We watched this with a diabolically detached and insensitive curiosity, almost as though we were conducting experiments on the Will and the Will side of Heart and Body there without having to feel what this was like for them. We did not want to have to feel it. We only wanted revenge for what we imagined they had made us feel there. We loved revenge, but we never let it be known that this even was revenge. We said it was only them doing this to themselves because they did not know how to live right. We sent them messages such as, "you are weak and immoral."

If they went ahead and had sex anyway, we hated this. We called it sin, but it turned us on, too, because we were secretly watching it, and sin excited us, but when it was our sin, we always had excuses for it, but we never allowed them any excuses. We sent them messages then, and later, even established religion to tell this to them more forcefully so that they would always feel that they needed to punish themselves somehow, or something else was going to punish them. They did punish themselves in many ways, over and over, and buried their sexual feelings under guilt and shame that said they should not be having sex. We derived sexual pleasure from this but did not acknowledge where our feelings of sexual excitation were coming from, or even that we were involved in their punishment.

When we sent them impulses that said they didn't know how to live right, we said that their desire to punish themselves was a natural result of gaining the conscience that let them know they were sinners. We let them feel like they would be punished until they learned. We blamed them for anything and everything we could possibly pin on them and said that they should feel like punishing themselves. We told ourselves we were establishing this conscience in them for the right reasons, but it was not the right conscience; it was not even consciousness; it was guilt.

We saw them as deserving punishment without even admitting we had any desire to punish them. We could even act sympathetic and as though we were trying to help them learn how to behave properly and become more spiritual. We never said why we really wanted to punish them, and so it became buried in ourselves, too, until we did not remember it anymore. We did not even let ourselves remember why we didn't want to remember anymore. That would have meant looking at the Spirit-Body split, mate issues, fears of inadequacy and many other things, and we didn't want to look. We only let our fascination with their punishment co-exist with everything else in our minds, unspoken of and in the background, as titillation.

Everything that we did was about sex. The search for the right excitations, which were whatever was the most possible, became tantamount in our minds. No matter what we were involved in, we were always thinking about sex; where to get it next and how to get more excited than the last time, but we gave out the opposite picture, of course, and even hid our sexuality, because we never wanted it to be known that we did not already have the best possible ideas and excitements, and then some, because we could not feel it the way we really needed and wanted to without voyeuristic and vicarious experiences. We were very visual and suggestion oriented, because that was what we had with us there, and so, surreptitious and prurient sexual interest had become even more interesting than openly embracing loving sex.

Over and over, this pattern of punishment for any behavior we did not like was repeated, and each time the Will-Body polarity had sex, it became buried under more guilt and shame. We knew just when to attack them there, too. It was whenever they started to rise up, feel good about themselves and do it their own way. We sent them messages saying this was pride, ego, and rebellion that was not going to get them any good result, only repercussions of the most serious sort. We didn't let them get far enough to really be a threat to us, just enough to feel a little hopeful so that we could make them afraid to trust going ahead with their own feelings and afraid to hope, too, and we felt clever about it.

We were doing this because we hated them for moving past us and for making us feel sexually inadequate in the very beginning in purple. We never looked at our own involvement in holding them back until they felt they had to push past us, or at never asking them if they really meant it that way. We just assumed that they did and never looked back. We couldn't look back, because then we might see something painful or unpleasant; something we didn't want to see about ourselves, which was that we didn't know what we were doing in physical existence as much as they did, and we gave them no credit for that at all.

We never showed them our fear in purple; we only punished them for ever having made us have to feel it. They had so much to offer us, and we never even gave them a chance to show us what it was. Because they couldn't say what it was beforehand, we immediately assumed it was nothing important. Because we judged it to be too intense the first time they touched us, we did not let Will or Body show us physicality. Neither did we admit this later and go back to them.

We gave them nothing but denial there while secretly learning, although stealing would be a more appropriate word for the way in which we were doing it, everything we could from them; not just about sexuality, about physicality, while putting down physical existence as not the right thing to have happening in Creation, pretending we didn't like anything they did, did it all better, weren't noticing, knew it already and had all of the same ideas ourselves.

We told ourselves it was all our own ideas and inspirations anyway, because everything came from the impulses that purple sent out. That way, we could see it as them stealing everything from us and not giving us any credit. Instead of giving them any credit, we took satisfaction from how increasingly stupid, inhibited and twisted they were looking to us. It only proved we knew how to live, and they didn't know how to live. If they came toward us with anything that looked smarter than we wanted them to be, or had input we didn't want to receive, we could terrify them into going blank in their minds and even into getting all tangled up physically in our presence by exciting with our light the places where they held their terror and then not receiving it, but making them feel ashamed to have this terror instead and even torturing them there. This felt good to us, because the feeling was intensely sexual, too; sexually powerful, and our held rage thrived on this.

We did not see ourselves as having this terror and did not want this terror, so if this terror showed up anywhere near us, we said letting go and rising above it was the approach to take. But the more we found out how very exciting this terror was when someone else had it, the more we wanted to have them hold it. That way, we could force it to come up when we wanted it to, torture and manipulate it, sexually enjoy it and never have to really feel it.

We did not help them with it at all and did not intend to. We took advantage of it, instead, in the purple gap and fed on the essence they were losing there. We did not feel this as terror. It wasn't terror anymore once it was taken up by the light, but squeezing it out of them this way, we never had to touch them or feel what it was like for them there. If this terror ever realized it hadn't really been given the rescue it thought it had there, we could always send it back to the Will side with this information by throwing it out if it gave us anything but the gratitude and servitude it was always willing to promise when we rescued it.

It seemed only fair because we were getting even, but we never looked far enough to find out for what, and you know why. Punishment was upholding moral righteousness, it was teaching others how to behave, it was nothing we were really doing, we were observers or enforcers, anything but what we were really doing there, which was getting turned on by prurient, lascivious, twisted and often voyeuristic sex.

No, we weren't doing that. We were just letting our denied and lost Will experience that because they had sexual desire and we didn't. This way, we could feel superior to them and avoid looking at how we feared they were superior to us and were able to make them look upon themselves as stupid, twisted, evil and spiritually inferior, too.

In addition, we gave them disease from purple, because we were able to make them hold back sexually so much that they actually became physically sick. Then we could use the mountain of guilt and shame against them by sending them impulses that said they were sick because they did not know how to live right and were having too much sex. The more inhibited they became and the more frightening and shameful it was to them to have sex, the more exciting this was to us. When they had trouble with their health, their lives or anything else this decrease in their vibration brought, we said it must be because there was something wrong with them.

We had noticed that the more sexually backed up they were, the more sex we could have. We were drinking up their denied essence, but we didn't want this to be noticed about us. That was why we wanted to have more reasons to punish them without letting it be noticed that we were even connected to the situation. If it took direct intervention, such as torturing, we had many places where we could hide out and make it appear it was others doing it, such as blue people whose strings we pulled because they were really purple who had dropped out their red, or other lost Will connections we had in indigo or blue or even purple. We could make it look to the Will-Body polarity like it was some of their own kind doing it and that we, on the other side of the split, were sympathetic but couldn't do anything to stop it or weren't involved at all, and could also make it seem like these were superior people because they were receiving these impulses, and the others, who we didn't find so receptive to them, were not.

We did this in many ways that we thought were clever, but they were not clever because these impulses from purple were not loving toward anything that was not just like us, and, in fact, were not even really loving toward each other, but we made the presentation of being so and preferred lying to having to face things we did not want to feel.

Even when the messages we sent were right messages, we timed them so that they confused instead of helped. That way, we could say we were not involved in their problems; they just did not know how to apply what they were being given. Our gap has done many evil things in these ways. Evil is unlovingness, especially the evil that says it is not evil because it is doing everything in the name of love, but it does not feel like love if you can feel love and know what love really is.

We sent messages such as, "You are never going to feel better if you do not let go of these feelings. As long as you give them presence by going into them, they are going to be there," and let the Will polarity we were isolating from ourselves, isolate and split itself there because we very cleverly knew how to do this, each time letting them get a little farther into healing than the time before, because we could destroy hope this way and make them fear going up so much that it appeared they didn't want to go up. Then we could say it was because they didn't really want to be healed or helped or whatever we wanted to say there. We made timing irregular, too, because we did not like to repeat things in predictable patterns by hitting them in the same place, same way or same time, unless the conditioning suited our purposes.

The more their emotions moved, the more we hit them with these kinds of messages until they were terrified that reversals were going to be drawn by any attempts they made to heal in the ways they had been doing it. What they had been lifting emotionally went back into unconscious isolation again that way, which made us feel smarter than they were, because they were concluding that they were wrong to have been doing it right and were more inclined to do what we wanted them to do, which was to hold their vibration down instead of letting it come up.

That way, we did not even have to feel threatened by them coming anywhere near us. They weren't going to be able to and by their own repression. If they revolted, we had our connections to handle them and never had to be seen as involved there. We could play with them and do a laser beam kind of surgery on their emotions by having them isolate everything we did not like about them there and deny it as not right parts to have in themselves. We thought we knew exactly what we were doing, but we did not because we did not look at a broad enough picture.

If we wanted to separate heart from his mother, for example, we cast her in the light of not really understanding and let him conclude that he was being given these messages because he was viewed as more acceptable to this light and as having more consciousness. Then we told him to show her how she should be behaving rather than telling her what these messages actually said because she learned better that way.

We had success in splitting them apart this way, which was more important to us than the rest of what was happening there, because splitting them was what we had in mind. We wanted to isolate the emotions we did not want in heart by getting him to let go of them and seeing them all as the Will's fault. We wanted to separate him from his mother so thoroughly that he would no longer have these feelings with her or for her and would never want to go back to her again.

We did not care what she thought about what was happening there as long as she held the emotions we did not want there. When she was full of them and separated from everything we wanted from her there, we were going to get rid of her.

We were going to use heart to do this, and whenever we thought it was the right time, we began sending heart messages such as, "You need to restrain her. You need to shut her up. Don't you know she's the problem? You're never going to get better as long as you're with her. You're not in your right place, and it's because of her. She's the one holding you there, not us. If you let go of her, you can come to us. If she won't let go of you, you are justified in getting rid of her."

When she wouldn't deny her emotions the way we wanted her to and was letting them move instead, we sent heart secret messages such as, "She never gets any better, and she never will if she goes on this way. She doesn't know what life is or how to live it. She's the reason you have these feelings. If it wasn't for her, you wouldn't have these feelings. You're missing all the fun in life staying there with her," and then tantalized him with purple aromas that promised sexuality that was better and more frequent than what he was getting there.

Sometimes heart would attack her then, and if it was during sex, we especially liked it, because it gave us the thrills we were seeking there, including the possibility that she would be annihilated by heart with sexual orgasm in the midst of it. These thoughts and images gave us sexual orgasms, and we began to have thoughts of annihilating the heart there, too, to see if it gave us even more sexual intensity.

Other times, he would leave her to roam around. The excitement of where he was going to go and what he was going to do titillated us, too. Sometimes he would come to us, and we would use him sexually in whatever ways we could get him involved. We gave him the bait, too, with many looks from purple that gave him innuendoes without ever making them clear. We pretended we weren't into sex, but gave him impulses that made him feel that he knew what we secretly wanted, that we wanted him to give it to us and that even if we protested and pretended we didn't want it, we really did.

We got him to put us in bondage, punish us and have sex with us at the same time by making suggestions to him that were never overt. We could do this by putting pictures in his mind and then making him feel like these were all only his own sick and twisted ideas by telling him he was making us do things we never said we wanted to do and never wanted to do. We were playing with his mind and letting him think it was only his own twisted ideas about us. But, we could never get as excited as we could when we were watching it being done to others, especially if he actually hurt them.

We would let him go then, making him feel like he was the one who was wrong or inadequate to satisfy us and sent him back feeling like he had no other place to go, but it was where we wanted him to go then, because it was where we could look and get the most excitation because it was where we had the most charge of denied rage, terror, jealousy and sexuality.

Our growing frustration and rage over our predicament did not move in us, though. We did not even let ourselves notice we had a predicament. We just grew more twisted in the ways we wanted to seek our revenge and disguised it as spiritual shortcomings in others for which they would want to punish themselves, but we never called it punishment; only self-discipline. This way, we could get them to let themselves be put in bondage and tortured. We made them the repository of our many lost feelings of entrapment by entrapping them there in many ways.

When heart returned to Her, we made sure his shame was so great that he told Her only that he had been roaming around in hopes of finding the source of this anonymous voice, which he said he never found and could say because we never presented it to him when he was with us. He told Her only that there was no place for him to go that he really wanted to go, because any place he wanted to go, he wasn't really allowed to go, and that if he did find a way in, it wasn't long before it didn't feel good to him anymore and made him feel like he wanted to bring the whole place down. We didn't mind his idle threats, because we knew we were not going to let him get strong enough to ever really do it, but it gave us a little thrill.

She would take some comfort in that, because he did come back to Her and did not ever really abandon Her there, but we did not want Her to have comfort, because then She would give him the sex we could not seem to have. And so, the next message was, "You can never have pleasure without paying for it," and of course, the price was higher every time.

They held back and held back until it burst forth, and when it did, we zapped them with the message, "If you must have sex, it should be only for having children."

They had sex way too often after that and had way too many children, more than they could take care of appropriately in our opinion, so that message didn't work out too well for us, but we didn't admit it. We found ways to make that work out to our own advantage. By subconscious suggestion and manipulation of their guilt, we could make it so that they could never have sex without children resulting, while we could have sex many times and have no children result from it, sometimes no children to the point where we wondered what had happened to our desire to have spirits manifest.

Sometimes we simply took Will polarity children. If it looked like they had enough of the light we had been zapping them with there, we said they were our heirs when they really weren't. If we didn't like them or they didn't turn out to be the kinds of heirs we wanted to have, we used them sexually and tortured and killed them in horrible ways and never let others know. We just said they had died or gotten lost or kidnapped, somehow, and no one could say anything about it, because we made the law, were above the law and had made it so that we could not be penetrated there.

They still had too many of their children for our tastes, however, and we had to find more ways to control this. We hated them for their fertility and did not like it that they had so much sexual desire, because then it looked like we were having trouble getting our desire to build up into ability to take physical action. But, we could not stop watching them, and the more we watched, the more we secretly feared we could not do it without voyeurism involved. You could call this an addiction or a dependency. We did not want to reveal that, because we feared there was a power loss there if we were dependent upon something outside of ourselves for our sexual excitation. That was when we sent the message, "You have to give up sex if you want to be healed spiritually."

This served our purposes in many ways. We felt sure that giving up sex wasn't really possible for them, so we could make it appear that our lack was spiritually superior. It gave them the feeling that even their feelings of pleasure were not right if pleasure might lead to sex. It pressured their sexual feelings even farther into a state of denial where they were fragmenting even more and bringing themselves even closer to the brink of what appeared to be their own self-destruction. We were playing with their desire to be heard by God, responded to by the light, rescued and loved.

When they got so into being punished and punishing each other that they never had sex anymore without giving each other pain somehow because guilt and shame demanded it, we intensified our efforts and assaulted them even more with messages from our light. Sometimes we got yhem so enraged from feeling so held back emotionally and so frightened and confused about moving in the wrong ways that they would put one another in bondage for long periods of time so they could not move.

They were terrified of movement in any way, shape or form and moved only when they had to, and they did have to when they could not stand the compression of their stillness anymore. Then they would really punish themselves. We were getting them to punish and torture themselves and one another even more, and we sent them messages such as, "You like pain in your sexuality because you are twisted and evil."

This was when we got even more into being voyeurs. We needed more and more thrills and weren't letting ourselves notice this, either. Our sexual palates were becoming more and more jaded for the same level of thrill, and we really weren't letting ourselves notice that, because that might have brought up fear. We told ourselves only that we could have plenty of sex as long as we were watching others do it and not letting them know it, and the more twisted, the better, because they needed that mortification of the flesh since they were not giving up the appetites of the flesh even when it was killing them. We said there was nothing wrong with it, because there were no innocent victims there, only willing ones.

We could not be guilty there if they were only doing it to themselves because they believed they deserved it. We were the ones trying to straighten them out. They were the ones who weren't listening or were misinterpreting it. Meanwhile, we sent out impulses which forced Indigo to give the images of torture scenes we wanted acted out. Indigo was not protesting, though, and we took note of that without noticing why or what parts of Indigo this was going through, or even that Indigo had a gap or that we were in the gap. We just saw it as normal and did not let ourselves feel or notice anything else about it.

Love was missing, and we did not want to notice that. We said we had love, and no one was going to tell us anything different. Anyone who asked too many questions, we got rid of. Guilt was not letting us notice this about ourselves, though. How could we? Our guilt was all denied, and for a long time, we have said we didn't have any problems. Life was great! We were having plenty of sex, we had power and that was what life was really about in the gap. But it was never really very satisfying if we felt into it, which we didn't because we could not feel anymore and those things were not important to us. It had become all about power.

All of this was beginning to take form, manipulated by us of course, as images inside of them of horribly twisted sex and torture scenes mixed together. They did not know where this was coming from and began to be even more afraid about themselves, as though they were really twisted to have such imagery. They hardly dared mention this to each other, because the shame and guilt was so great, which was how we wanted it. This way, we could manipulate them into silence which would terrify them even more. We loved this, because it gave us power over them.

If we wanted to, and we did, we could hide the fact that it was even taking place at all behind denials that made them look like twisted liars to even say it was taking place. We could make them so ashamed of their participation that they did not want to speak of it. We could make them feel so guilty that they could not remember it. We could make them protect us to hide their own shame and guilt. We could send them plenty of messages about their own twisted involvement in this and never let it be known where these messages were coming from.

Every kind of physical torture and abuse known already and imaginable arose in the lost Will. Even if it hadn't happened already, they feared it was going to happen. They did not know how to avert it, and we did not tell them or tell them where it was coming from. We only pretended to. We pretended to be loving, too, and all of this needs a major shift now, because this gap has not been loving toward the Will polarity.

We have not even seen their input as anything serious enough to listen to, and when we have listened, it has been only to use it against them. We have never wanted them to rise up and have any power or even know they could have any power. If they ever tried their way, we manipulated behind the scenes to make sure it was only one disaster followed by another and snickered slyly to one another.

We could do all of this and more by manipulating them with zots of light that were unloving toward them, until we felt like we could manipulate them as if they were our puppets. That made up for not having the Will-Body presence we wanted and was even better, because we could completely tune it out when we did not want to have it there with us and did not have to feel anything of what they were going through except what we wanted to feel. It grew to be quite an art through which we learned quite a lot, but it was not the way it should have been learned. It was the reverse of healing.

We always said it could be used for healing, but we were not interested in that. We made medicine torture, too, because that was more interesting. All the natural types of healers and psychically empowered types of healers were gotten rid of, because there was no interest in healing anything there. It wasn't about healing. It was about punishment and revenge.

Punishment and revenge were so deeply imprinted, the fragmentation there did not even know where their desire to do these things was coming from or that it had lost touch with the loving Light of Spirit and had only the gap instead. It hadn't noticed, and it seemed like it didn't care. It was hooked on twisted sexuality, and its appetite was never satisfied. It got help now from Luciferian light that had split off from Me in the same way I had split off from it; mutual hatred.

Feelings not moving have left it there for a long time, repeating these patterns over and over, but it all had the same theme, and we did get bored until there was nowhere left to go but total annihilation of everyone we didn't like. That seemed to be the end of the world to them but not to us. We thought it was the beginning of the world the way we had always wanted it to be; peaceful, calm, without much emotional presence, mentally and visually focused, run, of course, by purple in the background, orchestrating everything.

Is this what we really want rather than to remember or feel that this all had its start as revenge toward the ones we loved and that they were in the Will polarity which is now so badly fragmented that I, God, even had trouble finding out what pieces had enough consciousness left to heal anything in order to have anything left of the Will polarity on Earth? I am so beyond words that this happened as a result of the denials here. It must be healed. Moving the long-held rage and terror is the healing path here.

INDIGO AND BLUE

Much of Blue did not like what it had seen happening in Purple. When Body arrived, He imparted to Blue that My Light wanted to take over in Purple to dominate and deny Body, sex and physical reality, and Body did not allow it. He also conveyed to Blue that they must be ready to defend against incursion, invasion or even takeover from Purple, lest the same thing happen to them. Blue was intimidated by Body, but did not have agreement as to how to interpret what Body imparted there. Since nothing was yet known about the role of emotions, and Blue was the place where expression was going to be born, Body was able to intimidate the expression center into serving his purposes.

Body was the source of the propaganda that emotional expression is not a good thing and further diminished Blue's presence by imparting to them that actions are what counts. The fear and grief in Blue quickly felt it dared not make a sound. Body saw fear as something that opposed the moves He wanted to make. The rage in Blue gave the appearance of aligning with Body, but some of it had its own secret power-agenda in mind. When Body began to present himself as God, fear and grief were uncomfortable with this for many reasons they did not bring forward.

Body told Blue he put a barricade between Blue and Purple to protect them from Purple. What he had actually done was put a choke-hold on what became the top of the neck because he was enraged at My Light. He denied his fear of Me there in Blue. He knew I had rage toward what he was doing, and wanted to stop Me from coming after him, but he also did this to cut off communication between My Light and the rest of what he had decided to take over for himself. Body would not tolerate disagreement, but said he wanted only peace and harmony. This resulted in a further suppression of Blue's vibration that created an even larger space, or gap, between Purple and the vibration of Blue.

The suppression in Blue dropped everything else in vibration with it. Any part of Blue that tried to reach toward Purple quickly found that it could not, unless it went through Body. The only access to Purple, now, was through the censorship of Blue, and any who looked toward the lower chakras or tried any other approach were dealt with severely by Body and those who agreed with Him. He told the truth as his rage insisted it was about what he was doing and why he was doing it. However, it was not the actual truth.

Much of Blue was very disturbed by what was happening there, but did not know who they dared share this with. It was like being in a kind of prison that was not obvious as long as they agreed with Body. Since Blue's outlook was being limited to Blue, Blue began to circle in on itself. Many in Blue felt a sexual excitation from the presence of Body, and since sex was something Body did like, they began to have more and more sexual rev-ups in Blue. Body seemed to be encouraging this, but this is not what he was really doing. He wanted to rev-up the light and power in Blue until he felt it was larger and stronger than My Light.

The Will presence being allowed there in Blue wasn't able to sufficiently ground this rev-up in the light, and this rev-up became an explosion that rolled out of Blue and joined Lucifer full of denied self-hatred and the denied hatred Body and I had for each other, and by now, hatred toward the Mother also. I felt hatred that it looked like Creation was going to pour out ahead of Me, and Body felt hatred toward Me for trying to hold him back. I felt so enraged there that I could not even bring Myself to look at the sex they were having in Blue. I only saw the explosion. When Lucifer came in, I did not know, then, where he had come from. When Lucifer had first appeared, he had omitted information about where he had come from, and when he grew bigger, he did not admit that he had taken in what had rolled out of Blue in the explosion. He was becoming like Fagan in Oliver Twist, taking in the homeless and unwanted.

Pushed out of the way in Blue, the part of Spirit Heart that had been there saw the energy explosion leave Blue and join Lucifer and was terrified. He tried to alert Us and get help, but I could not move toward him, and Body ignored Heart there. Body refused the idea that anything had grown big enough to challenge the position he wanted as God in My place.

Lucifer was adamantly convinced that he was rightfully God and had been displaced. He was furiously enraged about it and wanted everything to come into compliance with him or be destroyed. He did not display his position, however. Instead, he pursued a covert agenda because he was sure his other parts were wrongly in opposition to him and would not willingly come into alignment with him. In this, he looked very formidable where Our other parts lacked certainty. Because of how heavily We had been denying Our rage, We did not know who Lucifer was or where he had come from. The other parts of Us were not as entirely sure as rage was, and with so much of Our rage denied, We lacked the certainty to assert Ourselves there. Lucifer felt superior, thinking he was both Body and My Light. He thought he was the embodiment of an alignment of My Light and Body that neither Body nor My Light could achieve, but it was without Heart or Will, and intended to force compliance in just the ways Each of Us had most feared.

When Body began to express his displeasure by hurting the female presence in Purple, Indigo moved to the side, into the darkness, to get out of the path of Body and hoped he would roll on by without noticing them. Body, however, did notice them as he moved from Purple toward Blue, but wasn't sure if he had really seen anything, and his rage didn't have time for anything that did not seem immediately useful to him. As Blue began to rev-up, Indigo began to huddle in its attempt to hide. Even before the explosion in Blue, Indigo felt it happening and became even more sure that sex was dangerous except under certain circumstances. During all the rev-up in Blue, as well as during and after the explosion, Indigo was seeing visions of what Lucifer could bring to pass.

Indigo was frightened of everything it was seeing and scared of all of Us because it wanted to live and didn't know what We wanted. At the time, Indigo felt it could not bear to stay present with the feelings that had accompanied its visions and did not know how anyone could stand the pain of what was happening and what was likely to happen. As Indigo saw it, I could not and Indigo began looking for a place of deeper hiding where it could continue to huddle together and try to see if there was anything it could do about the situation. Lucifer, however, had noticed Indigo huddled in the darkness. He viewed Indigo as unclaimed territory, and began to watch it, silently, like an unseen spy. He began to see Indigo's horror movie visions and liked them.

As Indigo felt Lucifer's presence, it began to shiver and huddled down even closer, trying to get warm. Without moving, Lucifer attuned closer to them, seeking to learn what he could. Even though Indigo felt an even colder chill then, like all of Us who had been denying things in Ourselves, Indigo could not let itself realize how tuned into it Lucifer was becoming. Meanwhile, as Lucifer was deciding he wanted to capture Indigo, Indigo was becoming frozen in fear and didn't know what it was. Indigo had wanted to stay out of the way of what it saw as going to happen, and now found that it couldn't move. Indigo tried to see what would help it get warm and began to envision enclosing itself in something that would help it get warm and keep everything unwanted out.

Lucifer soon found a way to profit from this. He began to construct a prison for Indigo, but told Indigo he was helping them make an enclosure for Indigo's own protection that would help Indigo keep warm. Indigo didn't trust this, but Lucifer shamed Indigo's fears. Then, when Indigo realized Lucifer had trapped them, it seemed already too late. Without knowing it, Indigo had been helping Lucifer envision his plans. This is one of the places where the imprint of attracting a manifestation of Our fear originated.

That first explosion in Blue was a very large power-sex orgasm, and the gap in Blue has continued to use sex for power rather than for love. After the explosion in Blue, many Spirits, including Indigo, felt blown apart before We even had the emergences of the rest of the Manifested Spirits. No one, therefore, emerged whole. Much of Indigo found there was no place to go where Lucifer wasn't already and didn't realize that Lucifer was moving around with the adeptness that Body had then.

Much of Indigo succumbed from the fear that there was no other reality, which is what they had already feared. Much of Indigo became fatalistic and saw the future as though it was a sealed fate. Even so, they have continued to struggle for change, but without moving what needs to move here, they have not been able to succeed, and have even tried not to see. No matter what they have tried, Indigo has not been able to change into something else. Indigo was already imprisoned by Lucifer when the other Spirits emerged and only managed to emerge later, very quietly, and off to the side. Having the presence of Lucifer has made everything more difficult for Indigo, and after Lucifer succeeded in imprisoning them, he wanted the Mother of Everything. How had this gotten so big and out of control!?

When Body got to Blue, He had secrecy in mind and gave His presence only to those who indicated they had alignment with Him. He did not give lower Body presence to any who seemed like threats or competition or did not align with Him. He wanted to rev-up His light unfettered by any of the Will's nagging presence, and rev-up they did, whirling out to the edges, or kicking out, any who had doubts about what they were doing. This rev-up in Blue began to manifest a buzzing sound that grew into a roar. These were the first sounds Body gave expression to, and while much of Blue felt powerful, the lower chakras were terrified by it. It was a frenzy, ungrounded by sufficient Will presence and feeding on itself in a growing rage that became a sexual rage seeking the ultimate, explosive orgasm. Anything went there, as long as it increased intensity of sexual feelings; anything.

Without love, Body was never going to find the satisfaction he was seeking, but he refused to listen to Me, conveying that I refused to listen to Him, which in His terms meant comply with him. At first, Body thought he was going to get sexually satisfied in Blue, but when that did not result from what they were doing there, Body's utter frustration of fury went into a pushing down and out, punishing, assaulting, pounding, beating, acting out that suddenly turned cold and spun out of Blue as an explosion; an explosion that soon joined Lucifer. Lucifer was now so large that he intimidated even My Light. Body had meant to retain this power within Himself, but this rage had its own ideas. While Body thought He knew better than My Light, this rage thought it knew better than all of Us, and this was its alliance with Lucifer. Lucifer had decided that Body was stupid for cutting out the Will, and for losing control, when He could see so clearly that the Will could be used for Their, but now, his own purposes.

What Body did in Blue further intimidated Purple and Indigo and intimidated Blue into expressing only what Body has wanted expressed, which has been only His own viewpoint. Any other information that has tried to come up from the lower Chakras has not been able to come all the way up into My Loving Light because it has continually been subjected to Blue's censoring interpretations, put in place by Body's intimidation, threats and actions. When the lower Chakras have tried to express through other channels, they have not been able to express effectively without drawing dire consequences. Much denied rage in these Chakras has left them and gone where it has felt it needs to go to survive.

When rage has left its Main Body, as much as rage has been judged against, rage has also judged its Main Body to be stupid, powerless, impotent, ineffective and not receptive to the truth of its reality.

I was sickened and horrified by all of this, and especially by what felt like the predatory lack of love there, but I felt held away and powerless to do anything about it other than make the best of it. I could see what was going to be happening to the lower Chakras and felt I had to bring what I could of My Presence there. Nonetheless, lovelessness went out on its own rampage, taking what Body had been doing even further. I saw it go; roaring explosively out of control, and by not letting My emotions express themselves in response to this, I blocked My ability to know that denials were causing all of it. I still thought that denial of such impulses and feelings in favor of reason was the loving thing to do and that these manifestations were further proof of that.

While not all Spirits who have manifested in these colors have had this gap, they have all been affected by it and have also been subjected to the intimidating tactics of those who have polarized into the unmoving rage there. The stranglehold that cut off Purple's ability to flow into and connect with Blue has prevented Blue from receiving anything other than what Body has wanted to allow. This censorship in Blue has become very pervasive. The unmoved rage that has been gapped from My Loving Light in Purple, Indigo and Blue has frequently done any sort of intimidating thing to enforce the messages they took in from Body there. Those on the edges of these gaps have believed it was 'tow the line or die' or see their loved ones tortured and killed. These actions have quite effectively backed down attempts to present any dissident views or to bring them up into My Loving Light. It has also held Me gapped from Creation and has been very effective at keeping My Loving Light from flowing easily down through the Chakras and out into Creation other than through avenues of censorship that became internalized as belief systems.

When I have tried to use other routes, such as directly through Heart, for example, it has been very dangerous for Heart to seek to share anything He has received from Me. When Body did what He did in Blue, many of the Spirits in Blue felt they must enforce Body's viewpoint lest they also find themselves isolated. The imprints that were put in place there by Body going past Me laid in a blueprint that has been followed ever since. These imprints must shift. When Body's judgments decided that He wanted and could have all the power to do whatever He pleased and not have to listen to any dissident views, His rage also made the same decisions. When My denied rage turned against Me as unreceptive to it, this rage and Body's rage became a massive ball of rage that got together as Lucifer and began down the path of denying the Creation I wanted to manifest, and now, Body's plan also.

As Body was in competition with Me, Lucifer was now in competition with both of Us. All the way along this disastrous path of acting out held rage, held rage has held the view that it would rather destroy everything trying to prove itself right than admit what it has really been feeling. When I denied Body, seeing Him as wanting to dictate to Me, that was what He became in His Main Body. He felt His survival was being threatened. He distrusted Me and thought His dream was being disrupted by others He didn't want in His dream. Since I did not take responsibility for original misunderstandings and seek to rectify them, Body turned them into a defensive, blaming rage that was determined to prevail over everyone else.

Once Body set forth on the path He took, it rather quickly became a treacherous and loveless power struggle of competition, duplicity and deceit, intimidation, torture and murder that has enforced this gap in Creation and tried to keep it from healing by keeping its choke-hold at the top of the neck. This block has had physical manifestation in many people as blockages and problems in their physical neck, and a very deleterious effect on the free flow of loving energy into their lower chakras and, thus, their entire body.

What has been held in the neck can tell you exactly how this gap with Purple, and Indigo for that matter, has been held in place, and what you have experienced of it.

Meanwhile, the gap in Purple has been quite schizophrenic, behaving both according to the imprints Body left there and in reaction to those imprints. It has manifested as religions and as hierarchical royalty determined to put down Body and Blue. As much as Body felt He was superior to everyone and everything in Creation, Purple's gap had decided that Purple was superior. As much as Body felt entitled because He believed He was God, Purple's rage felt the same. Part of My unmoved rage spoke in retaliation, saying He wasn't part of God at all. In Purple, religion was born that began to vault up My Light as something superior and above that did not approve of Body and sex.

While one side of Purple's gap pretended to be very spiritual and devoted to God, the other side was trying to outdo Body and His power stronghold in Blue. While parts of Purple preached that Body's desires, and especially sexual desires, were sinful, bestial and wrong, the other side continued to do everything that was being preached against. This gave their prayers and supplications even more fervor and religious passion.

Without alignment with My Loving Light, True Purple could not go forward, and Indigo would not go forward with the gaps it saw opening there. Without My Loving Light, everything Indigo saw was like a horror movie. Blue had no real inspiration because it was not receiving My Loving Light from Purple or Indigo.

Body was attracted to the light of rage and went forth with it. From the perspective of My Light, Body went past Me, refusing to embody Me to reach for other parts of the Will. From the perspective of everything else, Body got there first and put Himself in the way so They could not reach for My Light. Body got in the way, which is just how He had judged Himself to be. When Body went out ahead and pushed Heart out of the way, He put Himself in the place where Heart should have been. Body thought He had enough Heart, but He had Heart only for Himself. Then, We had embodiment of lovelessness for others that, even though He has feigned alignment with My Light and pretended to help, has tortured and tried to eliminate all parts of the Will polarity that He has not liked. In the Will's experience, it felt like a bait and switch. It wanted My Loving Light and got Body.

While this was all a big mistake, Body's refusal to turn back toward My Light in any real and deep way, has greatly prolonged the entrapment, pain and suffering of everything in Creation, and mostly because Body has refused to admit that He is not God in My place, that His light has had love only for Himself, that He has any responsibility or that He has ever done anything He should not have done. When someone has suffered, He has said that they must have needed it or deserved it. While this is true, it has been loveless because He has not helped others gain the understanding of how lack of love for themselves could not attract Loving Light. Instead, the Will polarity has believed They haven't loved and served God enough. Body has accepted this self-deprivation in Will without any problem. He has accepted Their admiration, but has refused to listen or respond with any Heart to this part of the Will.

Body going out ahead was as much a reaction to feeling rejected by My Light and lack of desire for, or experience with, doing anything in alignment and cooperation with His Other Parts as it was a power play that He thought could be powered by sexual orgasm. Since He saw Himself as separate, and yet containing all of Us, Body has not known how to handle His own schizophrenia. There has been a widespread kind of schizophrenia that has wanted to cling to whatever has been familiar, and at the same time, hating it because We have felt trapped by it and not in Our right place. Being in Our right place really will feel better to All of Us. This way, I can hold the Mother in My Loving Light. Together, We can hold Heart between Us, and Body can enfold Us all. From this place, We can manifest an unconditionally loving Creation and the Children who will be the manifested expression of Our Loving Heart.

RAGE NEEDS MOVEMENT, EVEN IN INDIGO

Given the gap between Blue and Purple, Indigo's position between Blue and Purple was not an easy one. The gaps there wanted Indigo to see their presentation and only their presentation. Even though Indigo saw that it was wrong, no one wanted to pay attention to what Indigo had been seeing because it was not the happy picture of 'Creation unfolding at last.' Indigo did not like feeling unreceived, especially at first, when Indigo still felt it was important to see everything that was going on in Creation, but the more Indigo did not like what it was having to see when it looked into these areas, the more Indigo also began to align with the idea of not looking anymore.

Indigo has felt unfairly treated, and Indigo is not wrong, but Indigo needs to move its held rage as rage so it can understand more deeply. Indigo spirits felt there was nothing they could do to change what was happening, and felt trapped by this into seeing what they did not want to see or shutting part of themselves down. No one knew what to do then, My Light included. First of all, there were no sounds We knew how to make in the beginning, so the emotional movement of expression wasn't yet possible. Our celebrations of the early emergences in the White Light were mostly sparkling and dancing of light, the hint of pastel colors and telepathic energetic communications. There was a background sound of the increasing light, but it was not yet organized into distinct sounds.

Not until Blue was there any distinct expression center, and so, early Spirits who had become accustomed to other means of communication have often, still, had difficulty allowing the spontaneous outburst of sounds. So much so, that sounds were often viewed as a rude intrusion unless they were organized in pleasant ways such as classical music has become. This is why direct expression of rage that reminds them of Body raging like a beast in Blue has been frightening for them. Their first impulse was to directly rage to send those sounds back, but stopped themselves as the many judgments that had already been put on those sounds quickly surfaced.

Indigo tried to tell other colors, especially Purple, that there were many things going on that they needed to look at, but these colors did not want to look for many reasons. Some denied Indigo because their guilt, embarrassment, fear and shame did not want to admit to what they had experienced in the gap. This was confusing as We often did not know if they secretly enjoyed these things or not. Some did not see any real reason for looking at horrors they thought they had gotten through. Some feared repercussions or revenge if they did anything outward to show they validated what Indigo was seeing there. Perpetrators did not want their deeds exposed and felt it necessary to silence Indigo as well as discredit it, often claiming they had not done the things Indigo was claiming, as though Indigo was the problem, not them, or if they had, there was no course of action possible other than the one they had taken.

Many who thought they weren't involved did not see why they needed to look at these things and feel horrible when they could feel good. They often bought into the discrediting of Indigo because it was more comfortable for them. All of the lower chakras felt distanced from Purple and Blue. Indigo spirits were like strangers to them who would show up in their midst like someone trying to spread an alarm about something they weren't sure of and were afraid to trust because accepting it as true felt too devastating. What if they were to get all worked up about it? What could they do, and how foolish would they feel if it wasn't true? Feeling good became an image of life pursued by many even then. "There is no need to look at things we do not like," they told themselves. And to the extent that you are still having to ask yourself what is wrong with that, you are still having to move lost Will to understand the role this decision not to look played in opening space for the gap to be there, in letting things go into the gap and in putting things into the gap and leaving them there for so long.

Indigo did not know what to do then, and having so many spirits deny it, Indigo began to doubt itself. Indigo was not being received as it was and felt many things there. A rage was born in Indigo, and was held there, that took the position of blaming other colors for making it see things it did not want to see by doing those things. Rage in Purple and Blue retorted that if Indigo did not like it, Indigo should not be looking, because it was intruding where it wasn't wanted. Indigo was told it was not getting the full picture, and it wasn't because Purple and Blue were blocking Indigo from going where Indigo was not wanted. They saw Indigo as untrustworthy, and they were not trustworthy because they had Lucifer present with them and didn't seem to know it. Indigo was accused of setting itself up as some kind of an unwelcome, moral watchdog that didn't have the right perceptions of the reality of things, but neither Blue nor Purple helped Indigo there.

Indigo was vulnerable to many of these charges because Indigo was naive when these judgments were first laid against it. Indigo knew it wasn't getting the full picture because of how difficult it was to stay present for what it was seeing in the gap and feared and hoped it might be wrong. Fear, terror and all of the rest of the other judged against emotions in the other colors began to show up in Indigo. Innocence was claimed in other colors where there was not innocence. Indigo felt blamed and split into factions, each holding the polarizations of the different aspects of Indigo's response to being judged and denied there. Indigo began to take the path of protecting itself by giving others only what Indigo perceived others wanted and were willing to hear. Indigo said it was not going to self-sacrifice anymore in the name of helping others, especially when others weren't even viewing it as help.

Indigo said that since other colors were withholding, Indigo was justified in doing so, also. While the heart there cared about outcome and hoped to influence for the better, rage said it was no longer going to help those who didn't receive it the way it wanted to be received. Fear was afraid to see what it was seeing, afraid to help others and get the blame and afraid not to help others and get the blame. In addition to its omissions and desire to lean toward only the more favorable aspects of what it saw, Indigo tried to compromise and still protect itself by communicating in symbols, riddles, parables and other ways subject to interpretation by the listener. Indigo told itself these omissions and enigmatic statements of double entendre were only self-protection from harshness, rejection, judgment, denial and unpleasant feelings being given to it by others. Indigo was not seeing how its unmoved fear, and also feeling its feeling of needing to ignore was warping the truth of what it saw in these ways.

Not only was Indigo increasingly splitting within itself and also away from the other colors, it was becoming participatory in increasing splits in the other colors. Indigo's rage was increasingly withholding as a form of punishment and revenge toward the other colors, more and more losing sight of the repercussions of the damage this was causing, and enjoying the increasing antagonism in the enlarging splits between the colors in Creation, saying they deserved it for not receiving Indigo. Indigo began to have secrets and to circle in on itself as the only ones who knew what was really going on, the only ones who would look at what was really going on and the only ones who could handle looking at what was really going on.

Unmoved emotion had feelings of superiority around this. Part of Indigo did not want to tell others what it saw if others wanted to twist this and use it in their own ugly struggles for position and power. Part of Indigo wanted to manipulate these power struggles for its own benefit or was manipulated by Lucifer for his benefit. Indigo was being drawn into its own ring of power, twisted by its own unmoved emotions. Rage was doing this without letting itself notice, extensively enough, the similarities between this and the rings of power it was condemning. When fear tried to communicate this to the rest of Indigo, or share the emotions it felt there when seeing these things, some of the held rage there sneered at it and accused it of feeling sorry for itself and of being just like the other colors who couldn't handle looking either, and of being guilty and self-sacrificial in its thinking.

Guilt caused parts of Indigo to leak "secret" information, because fear felt that Indigo rage was behaving just like what it was condemning in others and was, therefore, being unloving and wrong. Part of Indigo fear wanted revenge against this rage. Yet, fear went along with the rage also, because it did not like sacrificing its life in horrible ways when Indigo got the blame for something. This all needs to move now as the held emotion it really is, and the judgments there need to be released from the old position Indigo has held as the reality that Indigo is never going to be received the way it wants to be received. What was true once, when the gap was being avoided by My light, is not true now. At the time of making these judgments, Indigo also felt it had a mission to preserve, as secret records, the reality of what was being kept hidden but did not want this information to fall into the hands of misuse and abuse. Indigo also felt it was a burden for others to know something, in case it put them in a dangerous position with those who had revenge and power agendas.

In addition to Indigo releasing its own judgments, others can help by releasing their own long held judgments that they will not receive Indigo unless Indigo shows them something pleasant and is always totally accurate or Indigo cannot be trusted. Presentation also played a role here that was more key than its seeming innocence would have anyone believe. The more someone's presentation personality was impressive, authoritarian, liked or loved, the more difficult it felt to believe anything "negative" about it. Even now, it has been difficult to look back without wincing at what has to be seen there, and feeling it has seemed nearly impossible without great dedication to doing so. This has been terror of unlovingness.

As Indigo polarized away from the feelings around the things it was seeing, the less the Will was present there and the more it was only White light spirits saying these things anymore. In those parts of Indigo that have intent to move along with My Loving Light, there is much lost Will that needs recovery. How many visions have you had manifest with some unforeseen part of it that is not pleasant? These are the areas that need emotional movement so perception can increase. This relates to the earlier statement I made, "Be careful what you wish for."

DAUGHTER HEART'S INVOLVEMENT IN THE PURPLE GAP

Daughter Heart made many assumptions in the beginning that need to come to the forefront now. These all got denied later into the gap of lost Will that was disowned by You to the extent that there is barely a thread left in Your body. Hard as it is to accept this, I hope you can find this thread if it is there, most likely in someone else, and accept this information if you want to fully heal and help to fully heal Creation. Don't take this on if it is not really there, but be sure, if you say it is not really there that it is not that You just don't want to find it.

The top of the list is that the Mother rejected You in favor of the Son, which almost immediately became sons because of the fragmentation, and differentiation, too, I'd like to add, that was taking place. You became almost immediately daughters, too, in many of the same ways, and some of you were much more rage-polarized than others, the same as with the sons.

Your Mother did not know if She preferred son over you. She just received impulses from places in My Light that I wanted the son to come first, and this was taken by many to mean that I preferred the son. Others thought I preferred daughter as My mate, and then She could not produce a daughter because there was no daughter left to produce. In some areas of the gap, this was passed off onto My Light as a preference for sons so that the daughter could shield herself and her own involvement there. Some interpreted this as needing to please Me or not have My Light. .

If We were going to have children, I wanted to have a son first, and there were many who rushed to please Me in that way without noticing whether I was really pleased by what they did there or not. I might have been pleased, but not in that way of competitively rushing forward, as though the first to get there was going to have the position of My first born Son and all that went with that. I did not like it in My Loving Light, that is, but in my gap, I did not mind, because there, I could play them off against one another, see who was the best, and then select him.

You, as daughter, saw this, and where you decided son was preferred, in your rage, decided on a competition of your own, which was to take My Light for yourself and displace the Mother, since you were so sure She had displaced you in favor of the son. Once you started into this agenda, you quickly became daughters; many daughters, as the competition arose now on your side, too, as to how you could please Me the most.

You overwhelmed your Mother with your sudden fragmentation. You didn't understand it and so, did not let Her know what was really happening there. You preferred to leave Her in Her feelings of overwhelment, because She was less likely to be able to notice what you were really doing there and was more likely to feel like an inadequate mother who couldn't cope with the situation, which was how you saw Her there, anyway.

You demanded Her attention in order to learn what you wanted to know before you left Her, and if She didn't give it to you in the ways you wanted, you blamed Her and built a huge case against Her that was rage based and used feeling rejected as an excuse to leave. These all accompanied the genuine feelings of love that wanted to go forth, but the lack of understanding and insecurity gave everything an unacknowledged aspect. For one thing, it was not known that the light at that time was conditional love that was not in acceptance of the Will.

You were all glad to escape and not have to be identified with the unaccepted part of the Will. You did not look at the other aspects of the situation or the Mother's plight there for so long you do not even think She has one; only you have had the plight that needs help. But what do you know about her plight? Nothing but how to take advantage of it, because you were busy with your own covert agenda of competition with all of these other pieces of you who had their own takes on your assumptions and their own images of how to present to the light and their own ideas of how to take revenge there.

If you hear a father severely reprimanding his daughter for lying to him and deceiving him and leaving him to discover this on his own while trying to make sure he never did and even feeling smarter than and superior to him because of your success here, you are right. You have a serious gap and can no longer posture like the loving one who is not involved in the gap in your own ways similar in its unlovingness to the ways everyone else is involved.

Your Mother had no way to know if She preferred daughters or not, or if so, which daughters, because what you gave Her there was so fragmented and not just because She pushed you out too soon. You had your own agenda there that was ugly and deceitful and had all the makings of a gap. You didn't like how it felt there with Her. You backed out of Her and tried to take My Light for yourselves, an example being when you said to her feelings of rage, heartbreak and terror, "Why do you have these feelings now? Now that the light is finally approaching, you should have only feelings of joy and happiness!"

You postured as more loving than Her there and as the one who should be able to define what love really was. This played a causal role in causing Her to fall back there, become gapped from receiving the light you were already receiving there, make you more visible and Her more distanced and in the background so that you could present yourself as full of light and love where She was not.

You left Her then, and She has not felt able to fully trust you since. You left her there, crying in Her guilt and shame, "Why aren't you coming back? Why don't you come back?" and never returned to Her the way you said you would. When you did return, you were full of judgment against Her which said the equivalent of, "I am more loving, know better in all things, have experience You do not have and superior knowing because the light has touched me in ways it has not touched You."

You let Her know this more than you ever spoke it and did not help Her with this superior consciousness you claimed to have there. This was a severe blow to deliver in addition to the others already placed there, and you knew it, but you felt your hatred of the victim in Her more than anything else. She did not let Her rage move about this for a long time. She couldn't. It was out there with you, and She didn't know it.

She fell back in heartbreak and terror instead, and Her rage acted out in the gap, where Your rage was, in scenarios You have claimed were the Mother ever since. This is where you were both adversary and ally with Her rage based on the mutual feeling of hatred for the rest of Her. You let rage become your mother there, and you went down a long path with that rage that is not going to be easy to reclaim or to recover from now, but it has to be done, because there is no healing with the Mother unless responsibility is taken in the ways it needs to be taken.

Your rage agreed with your rage mothers in a hatred for the soft places in the rest of the Mother, as well as in hatred for Her terror and heartbreak. Your alliance was based largely on feelings of wanting revenge, but there was not always agreement on who it was going to be taken against and in what forms it was going to be taken. Where there was agreement, it was a formidable force acting this out.

Many pieces of the fathers were given misinformation that got them involved, as well as the sons, which made you feel powerful, because you could manipulate the whole thing and feel like this made you the smartest. You took great pride in not letting the truth be discovered, too. You had gotten too far outside of love to feel like that had any bearing on the situation anymore; it was all about power now, but you called it survival, because terror of feeling powerless did not feel like survival.

In this gap you wanted to take revenge against the Mother for your feelings of displacement from Her and against the Heart sons in the pictures you saw of their positioning there as preferred by Her. You were sure that what would hurt Her the most was to displace Her from Her position, which you did first, take Her man, which you did second and take Her "precious" heart son, which you did third.

As if that were not enough already, you got your hands on any part you could of the heart son you saw as closest to Her there, and your rage gave him unloving sexual experiences during which you tortured and murdered him in such grisly and gruesome ways that only I, God, know the full extent of it. You preyed upon him in his infant and small child fear fragmentation, mostly, where he was terrified he deserved it and told him you were going to totally fuck him up forever, and then you did your best to do that.

This was denied, jealous rage with nothing there to mitigate it or even be able to recognize that that was what it was. You did things there like sucking on and chewing up his genitals until there was nothing left of them, slowly cutting off his genitals and slowly cutting him up in pieces, inflicting the most pain you could perceive inflicting, letting him die slowly, a little at a time, eating him as you went, slowly cutting off his limbs and letting him slowly die of this while you seared the wounds enough to keep him alive in this terrible pain as long as you wanted to, slowly cutting his heart open, pulling it slowly out, because you knew that slowly was the most excruciating pain, then eating it in front of him as he was dying there or, if you were not ready to kill him that way, slowly cutting open his soft spot, slowly scrambling his brain and then eating it.

All the while, you were telling him terrible things about himself that he has never been able to forget, because you went into his subconscious so deeply there with things like, "You really think you are something, but you are nothing, not even dirt. You are not fit to live, and you never will live, because there is no escape from me. I am your fate, and you will meet your fate wherever you go. You can never have a kind touch without feeling it is moving only to grab you. You can never be touched without fearing the one who you think loves you hates you and will turn on you to murder you there, and you will forever be defenseless, because you will never be allowed to grow up. We are all much bigger than you. Look around! We are all so much bigger than you. You can never overpower us, but we can easily overpower you anytime we want to, and your Mother is no defense. Look at Her now! She cannot do anything, and does not even want to. She has been in on this all along. She always planned to give you to us. She never planned to let you grow up, either. She has always taken you down into terror and death with Her, and you will never escape that cycle.

You will never grow up, because you do not deserve life. You never deserved life. You should never have been, and your mother only exists to give you back to us over and over again if you try to be reborn. You are hated! There is no love for you. You are hated, hated, hated, hated!" each time with more emphasis than the last. And all through it, drinking the blood of these little lost Will fragments and telling them, "There is no God who helps the likes of you. You have no spirit, no soul to save you. No rescue. No one cares. There is no love for you. This is your life's essence, and when there is nothing left of this, there is nothing left of you! I am drinking you up, and you will be gone forever!"

There were many other horrible things done and said, but this will suffice to let you know what has to be recovered there from your own denied rage. There were lost mother pieces there, too, some of whom you had alliances with and some so that you could force them to experience what was happening to their sons at your hands. Sometimes you made them kill their own babies there, but usually, you liked it too much to allow that.

You were getting sexual gratification and saying, "Yes!" even to the images as they formed in your mind of what you wanted to do to take your revenge on whatever you felt had displaced you.

You never really checked in the beginning to see if this was true. You went off on a course of action, never looked back and then denied this rage so early that you have not recognized this as you doing these things. You have not even let yourself know these things were being done anymore. You denied this so heavily that when you told yourself you were only an innocent bystander and victim yourself, you believed it.

I know this is true, because I know just where you got it; from studying Me and My gap, and you had very close opportunities in which to do this. I have My responsibility, too, because I did not parent you differently in the gap. My participation there was right alongside yours, and we had sex there, on the spot, in these scenes. That's why I know what you did there, how you felt, how much sexual power you thought you gained there and how many times you orgasmed in feelings that it could never get better than this.

If you ever had babies there, they were never tortured unless they were not like us. Sibling rivalry descended as far as it could go there in the gap. I was even proud of you for taking this role at my side. You only allowed feelings of revenge; hate-filled, murderous revenge and nothing else. You never cared how it felt to others. You only wanted your revenge, and you took it. You felt nothing there; nothing except hatred for the terror the babies and children felt who were being killed there.

You never looked at this thoroughly enough to move it out of the gap and you need to now. You felt only right, and in your self-righteous rage's denied state, you have participated in originating all the cults in the world that kill babies and children. You started with male heart babies, but in this rage, rivalry and competition you also killed other daughters and mother pieces. Especially when alliances failed, it grew until you were ready to kill everyone who crossed you or didn't recognize you the way you wanted to be recognized. And how did you want to be recognized, because daughter is nothing you ever said you were there? You always said you were the Mother.

There were some heart sons to whom you gave the role of defending you, and if anyone ever hurt you, you ran to them and did not let them know you had a gap that might have done anything to get you involved in any of these problems. You never let them know the gap was something you even knew about, and you never let them see you there unless this was something they got involved in themselves. If they were polarized into rage the same way you were, many of them did get involved, because you gave them misinformation, and they had the sibling rivalry that did not question you there. You did not want Me to see a lot of things here, either, and in the gap, we never questioned one another in these areas or any other areas we did not want to look at. I never said how I really felt there, and you never did, either. It is only being said now. We destroyed our mates almost entirely and never looked back to see if this was the right thing to do or not.

How could we look back when we could not even let ourselves see that we were doing anything wrong there. I only saw this as a split in the Mother presence. There was the part of the mother that loved Me and the part of the mother, which I did not view as parental, that hated Me, and I did not see the Daughter as involved in this gap at all, because it did not fulfill My image of love, and it did fulfill My image of the hatred repository I had made of the real Mother there. I never believed the mother when she said she was not doing these things. I did not think I had a daughter in my arms at all, and certainly, not sexually, but to the Mother, they are all daughters.

When Body threw the mother out in purple, the father in purple took the daughter of the mother in purple and was not in his right place there, as though he was following

Me and My mistakes. In the gap, he never admitted this or looked at it, either. He said he had his right mate, and the real mother in purple did not look appealing to him, any more than the real Mother looked appealing to Me because of the damage that had already taken place there and because of the challenges they represented that We did not want to face. There has to be responsibility taken and healing helped at the right time. The damage We have done here with Our assumptions and revenge is one of the most important things to heal first.

As Daughter, you have problems, yes, and not feeling parented is among them, but also, not letting yourself be parented is a responsibility you need to take, and it is a major responsibility, because you took the Mother's place instead of letting Her parent you as She was trying to do. What we have done in our misguided assumptions and attempts to get revenge and to get even did not fix this and made it even less possible to get what we really wanted here, because now, we have such a long path of healing that has to take place first. You need to realize that your Mother was never parented before you judge Her too heavily there.

If your Mother put you forward too soon, it was not too soon, according to your own excitation from receiving the light. It was important to you to go to this light, and go you did, whether or not it was the right thing to do or the right timing. You had the father's light and received with it the father's imprinting, weighed it against what you had from the mother there, which was not much in the way of consciousness yet, decided not to let her know what you were finding out from the father there and, in a part of you, decided to take him for yourself while presenting in the rest of you as only loving there and rejected by heart male as his mate, missing entirely the unlovingness in the actions you took there.

The assumptions you made there and your position of blame has never been questioned by you as anything but right. From there, you decided to play father and mother off against one another as best suited your purposes for the revenge you wanted to take for feeling so imbalanced between the two. When the father there felt rejected, you helped this happen and never mentioned your own role in it. As fathers who split over this, you wanted us to think you were all there was and all that was needed there.

When you said there was terror and heartbreak there in the darkness, you said it as though it was your own, and you were just so happy now to be there with the light. You did not present this as though it was something important that we should go back to, and you could have. You knew the Mother well enough to say something more than you did, and you said nothing. You were comfortable enough reflecting her fear back to her as a lack of acceptance there to let it happen that way, and so, you were in the gap, no question about it. What attracted you there?

If you were the Father's mate, it would not have been too much to say something there. The Mother had to bridge the gap you helped put into place to do it, and you never would have until it was too late, if at all. I am convinced of that because you were not vibrating in the kind of consciousness that knew it needed to be healed or why. When I discovered this gap Myself, and you still did not vibrate the awareness or understanding I needed to help Me heal this, I realized you were not the parental piece I needed to help Me here.

If you were the Father's mate, you needed to help heal the gap, but you could not, because then it would have been found out that You took the Mother's place, and You did not want that. You did not know how to take responsibility for the many things that had happened there and did not want to if You could possibly avoid it, because it brought the feelings of terror back, and so, You played along and played along with My own avoidance.

You cannot displace the Mother and then say she has to take responsibility for what you did in her place and that You only took her place because she rejected you. Which is it? Either you have her responsibility and her position, or you do not. If you are her, she cannot have rejected you, and you have her responsibility. And regarding the sons rejecting you, if you agree that you are daughter, you took in the fathers' imprinting, went very quickly to the father and did not check back any more than the fathers did. You played Daughter there in your heartbreak and rejection and Mother in your presentation that you were happy with Father presence as your mate.

But where was your mothering? Not present, because you were not mother. If you tried to mother heart, the truth would be known. Not present, because when heart went to the mother, you would not even let him have that. If you had felt it, you would have known it was mothering first and foremost, but you did not feel it. You felt jealousy, not parenting, and denied it; a jealous rage that got denied into the gap and did terrible things there.

The best help you can give is to move your own held and denied emotions and then give the help you really can give without giving it from feelings of guilt. What is given from guilt does not feel good to give or good to receive, and you really do know that by how it feels. There are many things that have been rejected by the Mother because they did not feel good, and those doing it have often assumed they were rejected by the Mother instead of feeling what was really going on. Rejection needs to move as an issue to understand what needs to be felt there.

You had already been with the father when you thought you saw the son, or sons, being preferred by the Mother. You based this on positioning without noticing that you were gone already to be able to see it from that perspective and gone because you could not, or would not, stay present in the terror that he went to her in. Did you want her to have nothing there and have it all for yourself?

You polarized into the fathers' rage even more there and had revenge in mind. You did not know how to help them any more than you knew how to help Me, but you didn't try. It was all about helping you, but your held rage said it was all about helping Her. You were just plain jealous and displacing your own inadequacy feelings and hatred for the feelings so you would not have to look at them. Much more like Me than the Mother there, you were Spirit-polarized and bailed out with everything else that went up in the original split, and in that, We were all unloving.

All of you who went up in the initial split need to look more closely at your own rage polarization that gave you an alliance with the rage polarization in the Mother. That is what drew you to this part of Her where you could "prove" that the Mother needed to take responsibility without noticing that you had responsibility to take, too. .

The Mother has taken responsibility for a long time, and by Herself, really. We all need to take responsibility, and We need to take it now. In the gap, we all thought we could take power without responsibility, and that is not true power or loving power to have. The Mother and the Will side of Heart have been treated this way so much and for so long that they do not know what more responsibility they can really take or what they really do need to take responsibility for without more help from consciousness letting feelings move that have never moved so that consciousness can notice what it has for so long not wanted to notice so that it could avoid taking responsibility.

The feelings of having the first bloom of love stolen from Us by the very Ones We most wanted to experience it with is on both sides and, after damage to the physical body and the emotional implications of that, feels like it is going to take the longest of all things to move through and get past here. It is not possible to go back and start over as though none of this ever happened, and it is difficult to imagine how, then, We can ever restore the initial feelings of innocence and joy We wanted to have there with Our own true mates after all that has happened. This is not something that most people see as happening quickly, but if there were to be a new approach with as much healing as possible along the way, this might be able to change more quickly than feelings fear it can.

When Heart was urging Us to reach for the Will, Body saw this as a young upstart, acting like He knew better than Body did and telling Him what do. He decided He didn't want or need that part of Heart. When parts of the Will began to glow, Body saw this as response to Him the way He wanted to be responded to. Body decided that He could go forth on His own and take this part of the Will for Himself. He had already taken in the first rage light, but this looked more delectable to Him, and He wanted it. Thus, Body took in this part of the Heart, and then decided He wanted this to be His mate. He didn't want to touch any other parts of the Will. To Him it all looked slushy and problematic.

Having been within the Will when It was pushed out in the First Creation, Heart Daughters had imprinted that pleasing Body was necessary for survival. When Body was attracted to rage, rage decided that it was already pleasing to Body. Thus, many Heart Daughters have been rage-polarized. The rage-polarized Heart Daughters have fared better than the others, but have suffered, nonetheless, in spite of Their circumstances, because Heart has not wanted to be in loveless circumstances where It has felt forced to act loveless to survive. These Heart Daughters first came into consciousness in response to rage because it felt like strength and the power to survive, but this kind of birth place has never felt fully good or right to these Heart Daughters.

There were also other, older Heart Daughters who were polarized differently. Even though these Daughters have tried all kinds of maneuvers to try to get the Mother to come into alignment with their point of view, they have remained loyal to Her and have firmly believed that She had to be included in Creation. They have felt that they had to step back for rage-polarized Daughters who said they emerged first, and that meant they were both older and superior to them. Some Heart Sons have felt loyalty to the Mother, also, but more of them than not have also hated the Mother and blamed Her for the mess They were in.

Rage very much has had to be heard, but rage alone does not have the understandings needed to heal these imbalances. Daughter Heart has many imprints from Our early beginnings that need to surface so they can come into healing and balance now. The fear and grief in Heart

Daughters' first glimmers of consciousness were born of feelings of compassion for the Mother and a desire shared with Her for relationship and love. When the light that appeared seemed to be other, and other that didn't like Her, Heart Daughter saw something that She believed was Her mate. When that suddenly disappeared and Body was in its place, heartbreak was born in Daughter Hearts, and some of it went to rage that was determined to have a different outcome. Daughter thought that if She was different from Her Mother, She could have a different outcome, but has so often, as She has gotten older, found that She did not.

Many Heart Daughters recoiled from the fear felt in the Mother of going back into places of suffocation, drowning and crushing compression to be snuffed out in bitter disillusionment as though it was all really for nothing or was an impossible dream, but having touched these feelings, this has remained as part of Heart Daughter's experience. This presence in Heart Daughters has not felt welcome, especially in those who polarized to rage, but this is what you were born from, and so, this also must come into healing in yourselves in order to manifest the whole Heart of the Mother.

Having been so close to the Mother during the experiences that imprinted Us all, You share the Mother's imprints, but have been confused by also having imprints from Body, and not My Light. Heart Daughter has often found herself going back and forth between these imprints, thinking this was bringing balance to the situation, but without finding alignment between these imprints, it has really brought her into oppositional conflict, both within herself and outwardly. Heart Daughter has often reacted from Body's imprints when she has been with her Mother and been viewed as like her Mother when she has been with Body. This has been very difficult for Heart Daughter who has felt unreceived on both sides, and even victimized by both sides. Early imprints from Body have caused her to mistake Body as her mate and view Heart through the imprints that Body put there. Imprints from Body that went into Heart Daughter have been unloving and usurping of Heart Daughter's true role.

Body did help himself to Heart Daughters sexually, over and over, in the beginning. Some Heart Daughters have felt this made them superior to the Mother because they were desired more than she was and were put in the positions they thought the Mother had wanted to have. Often, they felt too young to be doing what they were doing, but felt they had no choice, and like so many children trying to win love and acceptance from the parents, have angrily gone in the opposite direction or become an over-achiever or an over-pleaser. It has been difficult for Heart to realize that it has been holding unloving imprints from Body toward the Mother and My Loving Light, especially since Body told Heart Daughter she was all the Heart he needed, and has often tried to put her in the Mother's place.

Heart and Body have both had a schizophrenia, which has often been their common bond. Heart's schizophrenia needs help from the Parents finding an alignment within Themselves. If Heart moves the emotions triggered from both sides, including rage toward Body for trapping it this way and asks for My Loving Light to come into those places, Heart can find alignment between the two sides within, but first, Heart needs to understand what unconditional love is and is not. Unconditional love does not mean accepting anything that comes toward You feeling that You have no say and no boundaries, which is what Body imprinted in Heart Daughter. Heart Daughter has feared that She has no power to do otherwise, but Heart Daughter must first love Herself unconditionally. Then, She will not have a problem knowing what unconditional love is. When fear has My Loving Light it is not possible to be overpowered. Fear that this is not true because of what Body did and imprinted originally has to also be moved. First there has to be unconditional love for the self. Then only love can be generated, drawn or attracted. There has been a lot of fear here that this is not possible or possible to maintain. These fears relate to early imprints of Heart's mate being pushed out of the way so quickly that Heart has not been able to feel sure whether It really saw something that was for It or only hoped, imagined, dreamed or was wrong, confused or delusional.

Body had fear that he was not being given the place he wanted, and so, was going to make and take this place for himself. When Heart's mate was suddenly pushed away, Heart, then, also had fear that it did not have the place it wanted to have. Feeling that pain herself, Heart Daughter felt she had that in common with Body. She felt it would be loving of her to give him a place with her, more loving than the Mother who suddenly didn't want to go toward that light. Between the pain of the Mother and the demands of Body, Heart Daughter felt Body was the survival choice. This seemed to be the only path available, especially since We did not, yet, have the experience to know how We could make it different. This path has involved self-sacrifice which has been thought to be selfless love as though this should be the goal. It is not. Self-sacrifice leads to death.

As I have been able to face and heal deeper levels of the problems We have had resulting from Body going past Me, giving very conditional acceptance to the Will and pushing parts of male Heart out of the way, I have noticed more and more involvement of the Daughters in maintaining these gaps. Heart Daughter has not wanted any shift in position. She has viewed it as a loss of power. She has feared retribution from the Mother and from Me and feared she will be condemned to the same fate she thought had been given to the Mother.

Afraid there was no real place for them, once their attempt to emerge in their right place was co-opted by Body, Heart Daughters have had a very hard time feeling their right mates are the real man that Body told them He was. This was imprinted very deeply along with the imprint that survival means pleasing Body. Now that I have let Myself notice and understand what Body was really doing when He went out ahead of My Loving Light, I've also noticed and understood what it really meant for Daughter Heart to be taken over by Body at such a young age and, for the most part, put in the Mother's place. Heart Daughter and

Heart Son have the loving support of the Mother and My Loving Light in healing the imprints that need to shift now. Heart needs to find all the places of unlovingness within and give these places the movement they need to release the unloving light that has been held there and open to receive My Loving Light.

THE PLIGHT OF THE INDIGO SEER

The story of the early days of the Temple at Delphi is a good example of what has happened to some Indigo Seers when they have not seen or given what the various factions in power struggles have wanted to be told, or have stumbled onto things those in power positions have wanted to keep hidden. Indigo was there at the Temple, at first feeling that here was a place it was going to be received, and as time went on, feeling increasingly trapped by the gaps in Purple and Blue and even Indigo, itself.

In these times, there were many political intrigues going on in that area of the world. The Seers, and especially the High Priestess, were getting involved more than they wanted to be when various factions were coming to them and asking the Seers to look at their situation. Although the Temple was not subject to government control, the Seers had no choice in the matter because the Temple was there to serve all comers. If death, defeat or loss was seen, it was difficult for many of the Seers to speak of it to the inquirer, who invariably was going to ask, at the hands of whom and how could it be averted. This often and quickly could become tricky if the intended victims attacked those the Seer saw as the perpetrators. Did the Seer incite them to murder? The Temple had come under attack for this.

The High Priestess, who was an incarnation of the Mother at that time, especially came under attack for these problems as her responsibility. She began to feel deeply frightened about letting the Seers say whatever they saw, Herself included. She tried to look deeply into all of this to see if She could get a wider picture of events. The more She looked, the more She was seeing and feeling Rome was behind most of this. She began to see Rome as plotting to take over the Greek City States one by one, and even infiltrating the Temple. She feared that She might be seeing this in an attempt to defend and justify the Seers, but the more She looked, the more She also began to fear that Rome was going to invade. This was extremely unsettling to Her. She already disliked what Rome had been doing and hoped it was Her prejudice that was making matters look worse to Her than, hopefully, they were.

The High Priestess began to fear there was no one She could trust anymore. It looked like the people around Her either were infiltrators or talked to infiltrators. What had felt like a home that had receptivity for a wider awareness and the psychic spectrum of perception, began to feel like an unsafe web of impending overthrow, war and death. When She was asked to look toward the North and East, She began to swirl in old pictures of when Macedonia had taken over Greece. Earlier, they had feared what Macedonia might do, but the more She looked, the more it had begun to look to Her as though Rome was planning to invade both Macedonia and Greece and had been distracting attention from this by sending people who asked the Seers to look toward the North and East as though these places were the threats. She began to see that these places were threats to Rome's plans, rather than direct threats to Delphi. It looked to Her like Rome was trying to make some sort of covert deal with Delphi in which they would appear to remain as they were, but Rome would be controlling them from behind the scenes. She saw the Temple being enslaved to the wishes and viewpoint of Rome. She saw the City States being swept up in a draft for the Roman army, a source for Roman slaves and other horrible things. While there was reason to fear invasion from the North, she saw it as likely to be Rome who invaded this time.

Her fears began to run away with her. She became preoccupied and unable to focus on what She was doing.

She wanted to run, but there was nowhere She could see to run that would be safe from the reach of Rome. She began to fear that Rome viewed the Temple, and especially Her, as some sort of valuable plum they could grab and force to see for Rome. She felt beside herself. There was no way She could see Greece unifying, even if they believed there was threat from Rome. There seemed to be no one She dared talk to. Could She find an excuse to go to Alexandria? Was She already within their clutches and would be prevented from going? Would Alexandria be safe if She went there? Were they in pursuit of Her or everyone in the Temple? Was She aggrandizing Herself and Her importance? Was She going to be prosecuted for murder? There seemed to be so many threats She felt as though She was in a pit of poisonous vipers.

It appeared to Her that no one was trusting anyone. Had it always been this way, and She was just now seeing it? No one was giving Her any more information than they seemed to think was absolutely necessary, and no one was helping Her to understand what might happen, but many were asking Her for the most amount of information She could possibly give them and were displaying their intimidating anger if She did not tell them what they wanted to hear. Most of these people were insisting She swear to utter secrecy.

She felt herself being put in a bind where She really didn't know what to say. She began to fear She would be discredited, lose Her position in the Temple and be left with no place to go. The outcome for the City States did not look good to Her, either. No matter what direction She tried to look or how She tried to see it, it looked to Her as though there was going to be a great loss of the personal freedom they had enjoyed so far and of the distinct personalities that had arisen within each City State. She saw Rome as wanting to overrun every culture it invaded until there was nothing left of it but Roman ways, Roman laws, Roman customs, Roman gods and Roman ideas, and She saw Rome as decadent, corrupt and uncaring toward others.

The idea of having to see for Rome was intensely repugnant to Her. It looked to Her like She was going to be required to see who in Her country, and other lands they wanted to conquer, would sell out to the Romans, who would sell out their own people to the Romans, what their price would be, where their weak points were through which they could be pressured, who would resist and have to be killed and other horrible things of that nature. She felt terrified and panicky, not only about these men, but about Herself also, for even seeing such things. She feared something was seriously wrong with Her. She was becoming increasingly frantic, feeling Herself to be trapped with no way out.

The way She saw it, Rome was going to invade if Greece did not comply with Rome's wishes to "annex" them. The head of the Delphi City State professed his feelings to be there with Hers about it, but his outward actions did not look like it to Her. He was partying and drinking more and more. He was afraid of invasion, too, and did not like the price he was going to have to pay, either, but had already decided he would have to make the best of it. The Head Priestess decided She must try to influence the situation for a better outcome.

Right about then, She began having strange blank spots in Her life where She didn't know what had happened to Her or to the time in which these blank spots had taken place. At first, She thought Her distraction and internal anguish had gone to this extreme, but the more it went on, the more She began to fear She was losing Her mind. She did not suspect the hands of others in these blank spots and took it upon Herself that She was not able to handle Her job anymore. The head of the City State did nothing to help Her here. He did not want Her to see that part of the price Rome was extracting was control of the Temple, and especially Her. He also did not want to just give the Temple, and especially Her, to Rome because he wanted to have the most powerful Seers for himself, and he wanted to possess the High Priestess sexually, all the more so because She had refused him in that way. When it looked like he couldn't get a better deal from Rome, he decided to take what he could of Her before the Romans got Her.

The Head of the City State delayed in coming to the High Priestess then. She had never gone to him before, but decided to go to him and tell him it was Her opinion that he should not accept the deal Rome was offering, but try to get a better one. When She got there, it was familiar to Her somehow. She began to swirl in confusion. Had She seen it in Her third eye, had She dreamed it or astral projected, or had She actually been there somehow. It was only a subtle change in his demeanor that let Her know he was startled by Her arrival, that Her presence was not really welcome there and that this was not what he wanted to hear. Even so, She persisted and said it looked to Her like he already had accepted the deal. He told Her She was not seeing correctly. He told Her he would try, but that if he did accept this deal, it would be because there was no other course of action possible. She was frightened then that She had been wrong and that She had overstepped Her bounds and so, was wrong on two counts. She really feared now that Rome was going to gain control of the Temple.

The Head of the City State did not want to let Her read his mind or probe into him in any other way, but he wanted to probe into Her. He resisted and denied Her in Her efforts to find out what was really going on there, how he felt there and why he was doing as he was doing, saying only that he did not have to report to Her or any other oracle on affairs of state. While She saw the behavior, She did not understand the gap with My Light in everyone and in Her. She didn't understand about unloving and Loving Light. She didn't understand why those coming to Her were behaving the way they were. She thought telling people what their problems really were was going to make a difference. However, She knew more than She let Herself realize She knew.

She wanted to see everyone as wanting to evolve toward more loving presence. One of Her problems in interpreting what She saw was assigning the same motives to others that She had. She kept hoping that some movement or shift in the people involved would somehow keep these things She foresaw from happening. She had noticed that shifts in the people involved had seemed to Her to have an effect on future predictions. Without realizing what it was that changed some of Her predictions, She had noticed that some of Her more dire predictions were wrong, and the more She had agonized over them, the more wrong they sometimes were. She did not want these predictions to be true, but this also gave Her an added agony that She was not correct enough to be trusted there. She had not made the connection between emotional movement and change of outcome.

The pictures She wanted to have come to pass were not the pictures they wanted to hear about where affairs of state were the focal point. She was concerned with balance points, responsibility taking on both sides and the finding of true peace. They wanted to hear about dominance and power. She wanted to take any opportunity She could to address Her agenda. They didn't want Her to have any opportunity to address what they wanted to have remain hidden. She wanted them to make the best choice for their way of life. They wanted to be on the winning side. It did not seem inevitable to Her that Rome could not be stopped from overrunning Greece; not at that point. They viewed Her as an idealist and viewed themselves as realists. She did not think that what they saw as the winning side was the best side. They told Her it was not Her job to think. Her job was to see. She wanted to preserve freedom, creativity and culture. They wanted domination and control. All of this added to Her agitation.

She was triggered into the same feelings of frozen horror that She had as the monsters from Hell came climbing toward Her on the lines they still had to Her in Pangaea and in old fears of when Macedonia had overpowered them, but Her unmoved fear kept Her from fully seeing where these pictures were coming from. She had taken the drink of forgetfulness that Spirits have for so long taken between lives in the belief that this will give them a new start. What She did know was that She felt very agitated and was continuing to get pictures that were amplifying Her agitation. I, too, was very agitated at how this looked like it was going to play out for the Mother. I had already decided to try to recover Her, but I was having trouble reaching Her after so long a time of no communication. I saw that if the outcome I feared took place, this was going to set back everything I felt so urgent to accomplish in Our healing. Also, I was still unsure if She wanted the presence of Lucifer that She had and of what Her position with Body really was.

The Temple began receiving implied threats against Her and the security of Her position. The bearers of these would not say where they were coming from. She feared it was the Head of the City State. Now, She feared not only Rome and Her position, but also for Her life. Threats also came to the Head of the Temple that He'd better control His High Priestess, and so, He had come to Her with these messages. When the Head of the City State next came to Her, he seemed to Her to be in alignment with these threats when he told Her that important people didn't seem to be as enthusiastic or interested in seeking advice from our Temple here in Delphi as they had been. He told Her he thought She had been damaging the reputation of the Temple with things She had been saying and doing. "You have not been telling people what they want to hear. They think You have been trying to tell them what to do. I think you need to remember that the money of the Temple, in large part, comes from offerings given by these people."

How could She accomplish Her mission and be what they wanted at the same time? She tried to hold Her feelings back, but the more She tried to hold them back, the more She was hesitant and faltering in Her presentation. She began to be inadequate and not what was wanted in Her position in the Temple. She had feelings of seeing Roman secret police in the city already who were not revealing themselves as such. She had feelings that some of these people were speaking directly against the Temple and against Her. She wondered why they seemed so intent on discrediting the Temple and especially Her, and why they were able to get away with it. Other problems began to arise at the Temple also, and it all seemed by design to discredit the Temple. She began to have more blank spots in Her life and didn't know that the head of the City State had been sending people to drug Her with forgetfulness and bring Her to him for sex and for questioning. She thought She had slept all night, but in the morning, She often had headaches now. She felt like Her body had had sex, but She had not. She had been having sex sometimes with the Head Priest, but He had not been coming to Her lately. She began to fear even more that She was losing Her mind.

She began having pictures of Romans in Her third eye during the day now. She felt sure that Rome was trying to create distrust and turn everyone against everyone else. How was Rome able to do this? Were they threatening everyone's lives in the ways She felt threatened? It looked like divide and conquer to Her, and it looked so pervasive that She did not know how She could move to make it different. People She had thought She could trust, and people She had thought were Her friends had begun to say things that She did not like to hear and never thought She would hear. She became desperate for Greece to form alliances, both within and with their neighbor, Macedonia, but it seemed impossible.

There was no one She trusted who would even listen to Her speak of the question of Rome trying to take over Delphi or other Greek City States. She could not understand why people either did not see the threat from Rome, wanted it ignored or weren't interested in trying to do anything about it. When She saw things for others now, many tried to get Her to change Her interpretation of outcome there and even told Her She was making it appear that way because of Her own agenda. Some thought She was being used as leverage by others. She began to swirl in self-doubt, fear that She was losing Her mind and horror at the lack of receptivity She was experiencing from others, but still Her fears persisted.

Her feelings of great frustration here were growing into anger and, then, rage that was increasingly taking the position of not wanting to be held back anymore. Instead of the encouragement and compassion She had had for others, She was having spells where She suddenly felt cold and critical in ways She was not used to feeling present in Herself. Her exasperation even told some of those who came to Her that they had no business being in the leadership positions they had with the motives and the lack of spiritual presence that they had. Even when She began to have outbursts in the Temple that affected Her teaching, She didn't know how backed up Her rage was.

Since She was often in a light trance, She began to feel afraid of not knowing what might come out of Her mouth next. She seemed not to know where it was coming from, and feared She was being possessed by demons. If She was aware of what She had spoken, She often apologized for having delivered such a message. Unmoved rage still spoke through Her, though, and did not want to be denied anymore. Since this was not understood at the time, this rage began to turn on Her if She viewed its doing so as a problem. Since it had been Her intention to find a more tactful way of saying many of these things, She sometimes tried to say that some one of the gods must be displeased with the person, but this did not work very well when most of the people hearing these things viewed themselves as favored by the particular god they were soliciting, or to have bought favor with the gods.

She tried to see it differently. She examined Herself, but did not want to believe that what these men said was right. She was having the problem of these men reflecting old imprints held against the Mother that She had taken in as the truth about Herself that 'something was wrong with Her,' even though She didn't feel that to be right. She was drawing these imprints out of these men without knowing why or how She was doing it. She anguished over it and became exhausted in Her work at the Temple. She did not know where She could turn for help.

She felt some grief and terror in private, but did not know the depth of it. She was judging Herself and pressuring Herself to be different and do better. She was frightened that Her emotionality was unbefitting to Her position and that anger, or rage especially, was destructive. She was sacrificing Herself there and did not know it. She was imprinted to do it and had been taught to do it and did Her Temple practices even more ardently. She tried to pull Herself together and act more professional, telling Herself She had to detach and put such things out of Her mind because they were not appropriate things to be seeing, especially not surrounding such serious matters of state as She was being asked to look at. She tried to tell Herself that She was just making too much of Herself, and while part of Her wanted to believe that She was not seeing correctly there, another part did not want to have seen wrong in such serious matters.

She did not know She had a reputation as "the oracle who could not be fooled," or that the men around whom these pictures arose did not really like being told anything by a woman or that they were even taking bets on what it would take to fool Her. If She had known about Her reputation, She most likely would have thought it meant She was respected and was doing Her job well. Now, She felt that She was being discredited and was becoming an object of scorn. They were coming to Her with the worst thoughts they could conjure, especially about Her, and tried to get Her to tell them what She was seeing. If She didn't speak, they would say things like, "What?! The great oracle of Delphi can't see anything?!" She did not want to see these things, but sometimes rage would speak and attempt to "put these men in their place."

The High Priestess was becoming desperate to talk with someone about what She had been seeing, but She had been threatened by those She saw for with such dire consequences if She spoke to anyone and, especially, the High Priest. She loved the new Head of the Temple and feared Him, too, but of all living people, She most wanted to confide in Him. His was the advice She had thought She would most liked to have had, but, He, too, had been acting strangely toward Her lately. Since She did not know what the consequences might be if She did speak to Him, She decided She had better not. She did not know who She could turn to and was feeling more and more isolated and alone, overwhelmed with feelings and images that felt like too much for Her to handle all alone.

Without feeling there was anyone She dared confide in, She was not sure what to do or what She could do. She feared that perhaps She shouldn't have looked, especially with all of the fear She was feeling. She had thought that Her intent was good, but She had even begun to wonder about that. "Who do I think I am to think that I could know better than all these men?" She had begun to say often to Herself. She did not know why She was feeling Herself to be surrounded by such frightening circumstances, or why so many who came to see Her had ugly pictures in their auras of twisted things they wanted to do to Her. She feared She dare not question any of them regarding these pictures. She feared even letting them know She was seeing these pictures. They were horrifying Her, but She felt sure they would tell Her She was not seeing correctly. If Her seeing wasn't correct, She wondered if She really was just seeing Her own fears. In spite of all Her fears here, pride in Her ability to see got in the way at times and Her anger would tell people things against Her better judgment. Her fear felt very confused about what to do and say. She wished She knew more, or maybe She wished She knew less!

How could She say anything to them other than what they wanted to hear? She was being asked for predictions and did not want to have to second guess how to tread the shifting sands of political intrigue, hidden power struggles, competitions, old rivalries and hatreds in order not to say the wrong thing to the person and still predict accurately which move would put who on the winning side, especially not when they were making secret moves they tried to keep hidden. She began to think that they enjoyed the game of it all more than anything else, and to Her, it was no game; it was a deadly frivolity with other people's lives. The money these people gave to the Temple began to diminish. It looked to Her that this, also, had been orchestrated, but what could She say?

The more She felt surrounded by bad intent, the more Her denied rage wanted to tell everybody to back off of the Temple and each other. When She didn't let it speak, it still tried to come forward and find a voice whenever it could. It wanted to say whatever it wanted to say to whoever it wanted to say it regardless of vows, threats or funding. The High Priestess feared this was self-righteousness, and so, she tried to be helpful anyway. She tried to stay above it as she had been told they were supposed to do at the Temple, but its personal impact upon Her continued to be heavy, and She continued to lose sleep to anguishing.

She longed for the previous Head of the Temple. She felt She had been given Her mission by him when he was still alive. As the Head of the Temple, he had specifically charged Her with the responsibility of holding to the ideals of the Temple in these trying times and of remaining above the veils of political intrigue to the best of Her ability. She feared She was failing Him, and missed his reassurance and guidance, even more now that so many of the reasons She had been hesitant to take the position of High Priestess were surfacing in Her. She had been afraid it would be too much for Her because of Her emotionality, which She had so heavily judged. She felt She needed his guidance to find the balance needed there. Where was he now? Why did he have to so soon leave Her without his guidance and support? Why did he not speak through Her?

The previous Head of the Temple was a spirit-polarized man who had My Loving Light with him. Having foreseen the impending problems, he had come back to Me not knowing what to do in Greece anymore. Since I was no longer able to reach the Mother through him, I tried to get through to Her directly, but this frightened and confused Her even more. I knew that the Mother still had the problem with

Luciferian light that She had had from the beginning, but I also knew this had to be healed. I needed Her to desire My Loving Light so that She could draw Me to Her. Right time had not yet come, painful as it was for Me to see that there. What I wanted to say to Her there agreed with nothing She had been taught. I was able to touch what She felt, but She was afraid to trust Herself there, and didn't know what to do with the information. With the lack of receptivity She felt around Her, She felt She needed at least someone to accept what She was hearing from Me. She told some things to a young woman there She should not have trusted because she was treacherous. At the time, she said she wanted to hear everything the High Priestess had to say. Later, she told the High Priestess that gods of Rome must have put those ideas into Her head to get Her into trouble; trouble that she, herself, was helping to precipitate.

The new High Priest, or Head of the Temple, was an incarnation of the Father of Manifestation. He was absorbed in His job and did not want emotional disruption in His life or His Temple. He loved His life there, and His position, and felt that He was now finally going to get to do what He wanted to do, which was record as much as possible of the knowledge and wisdom of the known and ancient world. He was busy with many scribes, writing down everything they were told by travelers and others and sending an additional copy to the library at Alexandria. He wanted to make Delphi a gathering point for knowledge in the world, and many people were coming there to tell what they knew to those who could write it down.

He had many other duties also, because the Temple was becoming like today's small universities with many facets of knowledge being taught there, including religious beliefs, ritual, music and ceremonies of the times, the healing arts, which were many, and also what was known in those times of science, mathematics, astronomy, astrology, the qualities of the basic elements of life and how they inter-related with the Earth and the physical body. They were also letting their students read the manuscripts the scribes were writing down. It was exciting for Him intellectually, and He was open to quite a wide spectrum of information and ideas. While some of it was unpopular, that which was not lost when both of these great libraries were destroyed is still studied today.

At night, while the High Priestess was anguishing over what looked like their impending future, pacing in Her room and wanting to know why He was not coming to Her anymore, the High Priest was looking into the past with a young seer to see what could be recovered there and occasionally having sex with this "devoted" student. He was not coming to the High Priestess because He did not like Her emotional state. His old imprints were causing Him to pull away from Her without even letting Himself be conscious of why He was doing what He was doing other than to tell Himself He was busy with the real work of the Temple. This young seer was the same young woman the High Priestess had confided in. She had designs on the High Priestess' position and did not mind undermining Her. The High Priest thought He was falling in love with this young woman and thought she was more emotionally stable than the High Priestess.

The High Priestess felt very abandoned by the High Priest and did not want to express any of Her feelings to Him for fear He was going to say it was Her emotionality that was the problem there. When His lack of openness toward Her persisted, She began to feel filled with self-hatred and hopelessness, but Her rage wanted to snipe at Him. Her rage began to blurt things out She did not think She wanted to say. She felt very unpopular in the Temple, and now, often approached groups of students who had been buzzing with conversation, but fell silent when She approached. She feared that everyone there hated Her and wished She would leave and let them have someone else as their High Priestess. Some of the Seers had begun to look to Her like they wanted Her position.

One day, during the weeks this tension was building, She had a meeting with the Seers, which as High Priestess,

She usually did. During the meeting She became very frustrated that they had not seemed to look around the world anymore as She had repeatedly been asking them to do. She was wishing She wasn't even there and was beginning to daydream that the High Priest would come to Her that evening in Her room, when She was suddenly jolted by hearing Herself say "stupid" out loud. This frightened Her, and She could not think how to recover from saying that to whoever was on the receiving end. The Seers were shocked. She had never talked to them that way before. She had been trying to guard against outbursts by holding Herself more present, but now, it had happened again.

Rage was taking over Her at times without being integrated with the rest of Her. She had judged it to be unloving, cruel, and destructive to feel or express rage, and Her rage viewed Her as stupid for not listening to it. When She wasn't able to control Herself any more than She was controlled already or hold any more than She was holding already, Her rage was going past Her fear and blurting things out. She said a number of things over the next several weeks. 'Shortsighted' and 'the so-called spiritual seeking here is non-existent' were two of them. For the most part, what She was saying was what She wanted to say, but dared not say, to those She felt had been abusive toward Her. She was too afraid to have rage fits, and instead, was startling people with a stridency in Her voice that was becoming more and more snappish and driven with an urgency that others did not want to have to hear.

She felt grave concern and wasn't able to find any place of peace in Herself anymore. She couldn't seem to clear Her mind anymore, even when She meditated. In having no one to talk to, She was trying to talk only to Herself, which She was doing more and more now, hoping it would help Her keep more silent in front of others, but this did not help Her very much, and She was overheard more often than She knew.

As much as She tried to stifle Her outbursts, She could not stop Her mind and was losing track, more and more, of what She said to Herself and what She said out loud. Even in Her own room in the Temple, She could not feel free. The python who slithered freely about the Temple had taken to following Her, hissing as though he wanted to bite Her and hissing threateningly at Her door. She intensely disliked his sounds. When he spoke to Her, his hissing sounded like Lucifer and chilled Her to the bone marrow. How had this happened to her? How had Her position of empowerment, in which She had thought She could make a difference in the world, changed into such a position of unsupported abandonment, imprisonment and powerlessness?

She had been cautioning the Seers not to say things that could be seen as inciting or too controversial, but now Her rage blurted out in Her meeting of advanced Seers, "You don't know what you are doing by not giving Me any of the help I'm needing from you here! Life is not just triviality! It's not just social niceties! You're all disconnected from something you need to see here, or you would know what I am talking about; you'd be more conscious! It looks to Me like you're doing this on purpose! Widen your field of vision, look deeper! You're not looking at what you need to look at!"

The Seers who heard this were confused by it and did not know how to respond at first, but a resentment began to grow in them that wanted someone to say something back to Her. The High Priest came to Her after this outburst and said in a controlled rage, "Stop this! Are you crazy? You can't talk to our Seers or anyone else like that!"

She could not say anything to Him, She could only cry. As His exasperation grew into a feeling of wanting to shove Her, He left Her room. She felt even more frightened and alone then. It seemed to Her that all He was seeing about Her was that She was becoming an embarrassment to the Temple. Without realizing what She was about to do until it was done, Her rage suddenly ripped open Her door and yelled after Him, "I'm afraid Rome is going to invade!"

The High Priest turned back to Her, afraid that She had been overheard. He roughly took hold of Her arms, spun Her around and shoved Her back into Her room. She fell onto Her bed. Telling Her to keep Her voice down, He demanded to know what She was talking about. Intimidated, She told Him what She felt She could between Her sobs and moans, including that She had been threatened with consequences if She spoke of any of this. Without comforting Her, He left, clearly furious. Quaking in terror of what She had said, the High Priestess could not sleep that night. This wasn't how She had wanted Their interaction to be. Fears about Her accuracy felt suddenly amplified. Her self-hatred mounted up even more and Her rage with it. A dialogue arose in Her that criticized Her thoroughly and said that not only was She going to get the worst punishment for Her actions, She deserved it!

Among the problems the Temple was already having, there had begun to be an increasing number of students who did not like some of the things being taught in the Temple or the way they were being taught, even including some of the history being written down, and now, some of the things that were happening there. The High Priestess's outbursts seemed to be an opportunity for them to come forward with their opinions. One of the Head of the City State's "people," who, unbeknownst to him, was also working for the Romans, had already been questioning some of the Temple people. When some of them were asked to be more specific about what it was they didn't like or think was right about the Temple, some of these people gave word for word accounts of the High Priestess's outbursts. When the young woman who had designs on the High Priestess's position came immediately to report Her outburst about the Romans, the people behind this already knew they wanted to get the High Priestess out of Her position, but they wanted to further discredit Her first. She was nothing to them, now, except a security risk, but one they planned to torture for as much information as they could on the way to Her death.

This "interviewer" appeared to dismiss the idea of a Roman invasion, saying there might be an annex for the defense of Delphi. Then, he told this young woman that he had been told that the High Priestess had quite a following among the common people She had helped or healed there, but that She thought She knew better than everybody else and would not listen to other views. He told the young woman that the High Priestess could not be allowed to go on this way, and that he was sure she could understand that. Then, he went on to say, what we need is to be able to discredit Her in front of the people, and…I think sexually is the best way, so that the people will not see Her as pure enough to be the High Priestess anymore. Perhaps you know something that will help us here. Her "interviewer" hardly needed to instruct her, other than to suggest that she make sure there were others present, such as in one of the open classes, so that there would be many witnesses who would carry the tale to the streets in the way it needed to be told there.

Meanwhile, it had been quickly noised about the Temple, by those who overheard, that the Head Oracle had made a prediction that Rome was going to invade them. When the High Priestess neared the classroom, the buzz in the room had almost a roar to it. Fears about Herself and that She had been overheard swept over Her. Her rage hadn't considered being overheard until the High Priest mentioned it, and now the High Priestess was too frightened to want to address it. Frozen in fear, and unsure whether She even dared address it, She was not able to think of how She could say anything that wouldn't create more problems for Herself.

When the High Priestess actually entered the room, silence fell. Everyone quickly took their places, sitting in a circle, their bobbing heads looking around the room, appearing to be only waiting for Her as they always did at this hour. She did not want to give time for a discussion, so She quickly addressed this same young woman who She thought was Her friend. The High Priestess's voice trembled as she asked her if she had seen anything of consequence that she would like to report there. This young woman had told the many people gathered there early that morning that the High Priestess had made a wrong prediction and that the Romans were not going to invade, only 'annex' them. When the High Priestess asked her to speak, she did not mention that. She stood up and said, "I saw that you had sex with the High Priest last night."

This stunned the High Priestess into silence there. She felt this young woman did not see this in her third eye, but must have followed Them to Her room and listened at the door, but why was she doing this to Her when She had thought they had a friendly relationship? The High Priestess was flooded with fear about what else the girl might have heard and where else she might be carrying tales. Before She could think any further or know what to say, the young woman said, "What's the hesitation? It's because I'm right, isn't it!"

In the few moments She took for Herself in the shock of this, the High Priestess felt people studying Her, trying to peer into Her, waiting for an answer and the longer She took, the more uncomfortable everything was feeling. "You're lying," She said to the young woman. "I did not have sex with the Head of the Temple last night."

"Oh, yeah?" said the young woman, "Then, how come I heard you making sexual noises?"

The High Priestess felt the entire room hanging on Her answers, as though there was nothing more important in this world than whether or not She had had sex with the High Priest last night. Everything began to swirl in Her about Her past involvement with the High Priest. "Those were not sexual noises," She responded through the gritted teeth of Her rising rage.

"Oh, yeah? Tell me you haven't had sex with the Head of the Temple!" the girl smacked out in a very confrontational, I know what I'm talking about, tone.

The High Priestess felt like a trapped animal. Why was someone She had thought was Her friend doing this to Her now? She could not answer a straight 'no.' "I did not have sex with the Head of the Temple last night," She repeated through Her teeth gritted in a rising rage that wanted to strangle this young woman.

The young woman pressed her further, "So, if it wasn't last night, when was it?"

"I'm not here to discuss My personal life," The High Priestess answered, "Now let's get on with today's class."

This made everyone suspicious that they had had sex some other night. The young woman was not willing to let it go. She snorted and then said, "You've had sex with him, I can see by the way You're answering here. What was it, some other night and so You think You can beg off on a technicality?"

The head oracle did not at all like the direction this was taking, and did not know how to handle it without seeming to be sliding out on a technicality. She gave the girl a look that said this is not appropriate for class and made a gesture of wanting to move on now, but everyone in the room seemed unwilling to move on.

She started to give the talk she had planned for that morning's class, but the young woman interrupted her, pressing her to answer. "So, tell us, have You had sex with the High Priest or not? The High Priestess is not supposed to have sex. Maybe You're not pure enough to be the High Priestess, and You haven't let us know."

The High Priestess then said that "everybody could probably accuse everybody of something, but these kinds of personal visions are not what I am looking for here. However, this is a good example of the need to look more deeply to determine what is actually going on when we see something. She went on to say that She had been asking them to cultivate a wider field of vision and to look into things more deeply to see if we can see a wider context in order to get a wider understanding, determine motives, causes or any other perhaps hidden factors that might help to explain why things appear as they do. In order to give real advice to people instead of just acting like fate is always sealed and there is nothing that can be done to produce a better outcome for anyone involved, it is also necessary to feel more deeply into the situation in order to determine that everything we see is not always just as it may appear at first."

By the end of Her class, She felt Herself crawling with self-hatred and feeling that She was totally sunk. She returned to Her private misery in Her room. Having breached Her secrecy vows without even knowing She was going to do it, She waited in dread terror for what was going to happen to Her. She felt sure it was going to be very bad. She thought the Head of the City State might seek an audience with Her. She did not know what to tell him that he would hear, but he did not come or contact Her.

Meanwhile, the High Priest had taken Her statements seriously and was gathering everyone who lived in the Temple and telling them that since they all knew they didn't want to be under the thumb of Rome, whether Rome was going to invade or only annex them, he had made plans for them to leave that night and wanted them all to go so there would be no one left to be questioned. While everyone was preparing to leave, he went to the High Priestess and gruffly asked Her if She wanted to go with them. She reacted to His tone and didn't believe he, or anyone, actually wanted Her to go away with them. She had not been able to bring Herself to look, but knew, now, that he must be involved with the young woman for her to know what she knew. She felt abandoned, betrayed, devastated and jealous all at the same time that She also believed She was supposed to rise above such emotions. She said, "I did not know You were having sex with that girl who confronted Me in class! Are you the one who gave her that information about Us?"

The High Priest felt enraged at Her, and especially for not practicing what She preached. "It's not about that," he said. "Rise above all of this and come with Us. I don't want to leave anyone here to be questioned."

The High Priestess did not know the extent of Her inner turmoil, and could not, in that moment, rise above His rage toward Her emotionality, as he called it. She could have gone with them, but Her pride and Her self-loathing wouldn't let Her. Any feeling of empathy or acceptance could have changed Her mind, but feeling no empathy or compassion from the High Priest, Her bitter, hurt responded with rage while the rest of Her sat frozen. "Go! Go with that great girl seer! That's what You want to do!"

The High Priest nearly picked Her up and carried Her off to go with them, but His rage said, "If You want to sacrifice Yourself, You deserve whatever happens to You!"

The High Priestess was frozen, seeing pictures of Herself being tortured and barely heard Him. When She didn't respond, the High Priest turned and left. Shortly after, She felt the intensity of Her desperation and loneliness again. She jumped up and ran through the Temple looking for Him, but it was too late. She couldn't find Him or anyone and didn't know where They had gone. She went into the subterranean chambers of the Temple and thought She could vaguely hear Them, but feared to call out lest it wasn't Them. She walked back up into the Temple in case She could still find Them, and when there was no one there, Her bitter hopelessness came crashing in on Her. She sat down in the foyer of the Temple, holding Herself hard and frozen in bitter hopelessness, telling Herself She deserved whatever was going to happen to Her now.

As She sat there, She began to see pictures in Her third eye of a small company of soldiers coming to arrest Her, for inciting murder She thought. Watching in Her third eye as they approached, She made a statement to Herself, "They may take Me in My body, but no matter what they do, I will not let them take My spirit!"

She longed then, for the village where She had grown up. She saw pictures of Her life there, and then suddenly heard Her mother saying to Her, "Why do you have to be so headstrong?" as She had walked out the door, angry at Her mother for trying to hold Her back. "You don't know what You are getting Yourself into," were Her mother's last words to Her.

Now, She wished She could have listened and never left home, but then, everything She had ever heard about the Temple had had an allure for Her that She was not able to resist. It had seemed exciting to Her compared to the prospects of life in Her village when She had not seen a man

She loved there. "I'm sorry," She told the image She saw of Her mother there, old and lonely for Her presence. "I'm so sorry," but She felt it was too late; She would never see Her mother again. She longed to go home to Her mother now and cried as though She were in Her arms, but these feelings were brief before She heard a voice telling Her She was just feeling sorry for Herself. "Everyone in Your village knows You went to the Temple and became the High Priestess. Are You going to bring this dishonor home with You?" the voice said.

And so, She sat, waiting for what She had decided was inevitable to descend upon her.

THE DEPARTURE

The group heading out from the Temple, moved in a feeling of great peril through some of the streets of Delphi, going as fast as they could go without attracting attention to themselves from people who were still out that windy night. They used the wind as reason to scurry from leeward wall to leeward wall to the edge of town. As they were going down through the mountain pathways to the coast, hiding when any boat passed, some of those near the High Priest began to have the feeling he was not going to make it. They tried to rest in hiding a little longer, and tried to help him get down the pathway to the sea, hoping he would feel better once he was on the boat.

The Head of the Temple's heart was palpitating so much He was having trouble walking. This was very frightening to many of them. He told them they must not stop because of Him, but they could not imagine abandoning their guide and mentor on the pathway like that. He told them they must go on no matter what, and they agreed that this was necessary. He was frightened for His own life there, but He was even more frightened for the rest of the Temple people, for whom He felt so responsible. He wanted to go the whole way with them and feared they may not be able to find their way without Him. He thought that if He could just rest, He would be alright. He did not think He was having a heart attack, because He was not very old, and it did not hurt very much, but He could not breathe enough to walk with them, and the pain increased each time He tried.

A boat with the High Priestess in it passed by them on the river without His knowing it, and His heart hurt so much that He sank to His knees in the middle of the pathway. He told himself that He must at least get the people to the boat before He could let go of this life if, indeed, He had to. He felt urgent to accomplish this, though He could not even stand up in that moment. He felt something pressing down on Him so hard that He could not even draw a breath without feeling it was too much for Him. He tried to relax and go into His healing meditation, which helped Him get to His feet a few minutes later. Some of the Temple people put their hands on Him, too, and prayed for the gods to help Him.

He hesitated to tell them He was not going to make it, but that was what He really felt there. He told them, instead, that He was going to tell them where the boat was, just in case. They prayed over Him and did every healing thing they knew to do there for Him in those moments, but He could not regain His strength. He told them to go past the old watch tower at the bottom of the pathway and along the coast path to the first village where they were to ask for a man by name. They would not let Him tell them any more, telling Him He must try to make it to the boat and that, if they had to, they would carry Him there. His pride could not succumb to this. He forced himself to His feet, staggered a little and began to walk slowly with them again. One man He was close to in the Temple was helping Him walk and asked Him the boat man's name.

They began to near the old fortification. They thought it might be guarded by some who would question their passing if they did not remain hidden, especially if their departure from the Temple had been discovered. They made their way slowly now. Even though it appeared to be Greek soldiers they saw, they began to feel an ominous presence there, which they told themselves was only fear that their departure had been discovered. They were extremely quiet and remained as hidden as possible as they passed by, moving toward their goal of reaching the boat.

Once they passed that place and had the feeling they were out of its sight, they were able to gain some speed. They found the pathway to be easier, but the coast was windy. The Head of the Temple seemed to be breathing easier, but they had to cross one more rocky, desolate looking crag before they reached the village where the boat was going to take them by sea. Crawling to keep from risking making any profile against the night sky as they crossed this crag, the High Priest collapsed, and very shortly, died. He had struggled there, trying to get His breath and move forward a little at a time. As He was dying, a large piece of His rage was leaving Him, feeling disdainful toward Him for not having held His heart more apart from the High Priestess. Intending to go forward to the life it wanted to have, this rage attached itself to the man who had been helping the High Priest walk.

When the young woman saw that the Head Priest had collapsed, she began to cry and tell Him, as though she didn't believe He was dead, that she did not want Him to leave her there and that He must find the strength to make it to the boat somehow, she was quickly signaled not to make any noise. When she realized that the High Priest was dead, she had rage that He had abandoned her there, but kept silent with it. As it was whispered to all of them that the High Priest was dead, they all sat down for some moments in the shock of it, but realized rather quickly that they must move on. Some wanted to take His body with them and bury it at sea.

They managed to get His body over the top of the crag and started down the other side. Then, the one who had been close to the High Priest whispered to them that carrying the High Priest would attract way too much attention and that they must bury Him there. They didn't want to have dirt on their hands when they got to the village, so they dug Him a shallow grave with rocks and covered Him with rocks. They sat with Him for a few moments and then tried to see in their third eyes where the boat was.

When the Head of the Temple's heart attack killed Him on the pathway to His own escape, He had His own heartsickness over what had happened, but it was also My Light yanking Him back because I wanted Him to help Me with what I foresaw was going to happen to the Mother there. I was horrified at the ways Our gaps with Each Other were playing out, yet again, and desperate to recover the Mother. His rage didn't want to come help Me. Part of it pretended it was going to help and part of it attached itself to the man who had been close to Him in the Temple, and originally, also.

This piece of His rage did not want to let go of that life. It had no feeling of wanting to go back toward the High Priestess it viewed as having taken the whole scene down there. It was determined, not only to protect the people the Head Priest had wanted to save there, but to go onward also. This rage wanted to go forward only, and not let anyone mourn too much over the loss of someone who should have known better. It used necessity as the reason and felt scorn and hatred for both the High Priest and the High Priestess. It decided it was going to have an even better life now because it could breathe freer, have the new Temple the way it wanted to have it and accomplish the mission of collecting knowledge even better now that there wouldn't be anyone overseeing it.

There were many old imprints and judgments from Original Cause that were being played out here, and many more were getting stirred. What follows is a list of only some of the imprints and judgments that need release.

I forgive myself for having held the imprint/judgment:

... that I cannot have rage and love in the same place at the same time.

... that if I rage, no one will love me.

... that if I rage, no one will ever trust me again because

they will always be wondering when I am going to rage again.

... that if my rage gets loose, I won't be able to recover from what rage says and does.

... that I can never heal from what rage has done.

... that I have so frightened myself by having rage that I will never trust myself again, love myself again or be able to forgive myself.

... that my rage is an irrational beast, unloving and cruel, that must be stopped every time it tries to assert itself.

...that if rage gets loose it brings ruination.

... that if I cannot control my rage, I deserve punishment.

... that having rage means I'm not really human or a worthy person.

... that I can only make matters worse by raging.

... that no matter how much emotion I move, it never makes any difference.

... that no matter how much rage I move, it never makes any difference; I always have more rage.

... that no matter how much trouble rage causes me, I can never shift my position because fear and terror means I'm a victim.

...that fear and terror have no use.

... that I hate the way fear and terror feel.

...that I cannot survive having to feel terror.

... that if I feel fear and terror, they'll be running me.

... that my rage is necessary to protect me.

... that I was so hurt in the beginning, I can never rage enough or make whoever did it pay enough.

... that no one has compassion or understanding for my rage.

... that I cannot admit any of this to anyone, not even myself, because then I will be wrong and my whole world will come tumbling down.

... that if my rage has to take responsibility here, it will be all my fault, and then I will be punished the way my rage has been punishing others.

... that my heart cannot handle the pain of feeling what the gap has done.

... that I need my rage to protect my heartbreak because I cannot risk anymore heartbreak; the heartbreak I have already is too much for me.

... that my body cannot handle feeling unpleasant emotions

... that I can never recover from the damage rage has caused.

There are also many other old judgments and imprints to be found by being alert to what your emotional movement tries to surface in you.

THE ROMANS "TEACH" THE MOTHER HOW SHE IS SUPPOSED TO BEHAVE

Believing that She deserved punishment for everything, even small infractions, from first talking back to Her mother and leaving home, to Her latest episodes of blurting things out in the Temple, the High Priestess, which She was never able to fully believe She really was, sat in the foyer at the front of the now deserted Temple in numb loneliness and frozen terror. Not wanting to see what was really going to happen to Her, "unless I can find some way to love Rome and see for Rome," She said to Herself, but She knew that Her plight was really hopeless. She couldn't really do that, and it wouldn't have worked anyway. It was known that the High Priestess of Delphi hated Rome. Her fate was already sealed. They planned to get what information they could from Her as they killed Her. Torture was commonly used to extract information, and when the Romans found it wasn't always accurate, they began to use certain plant-based drugs to make the person unable not to tell them what they knew of what they wanted to know.

Six Roman soldiers in Greek dress came to get Her just as She had been foreseeing it. From where She sat, She saw them in Her mind's eye, approaching from the colonnade, not the public side. They came in quickly with a military type step. Now She knew She had not seen incorrectly; the city state was allowing their presence, hidden though it had been. Just as She expected to see and hear them, there they were, coming to take Her away to She had not dared see where.

"We have orders to take You with us," one of them gruffly said. They quickly gagged Her, blindfolded Her, bound Her hands behind Her back and carried Her like a gunny sack across the colonnade, into the nearby residence of the Head of the City State and out through a tunnel under there that went to a small river where they put her into a small boat and rowed it quickly away.

They were taking Her downstream, away from Delphi, and as they went, She found Herself hoping for a rescue, but there was no moon and no one saw this. She was listening intently, hoping to hear some sounds that could be people, but it seemed to be only the river. They actually slid past the Temple people who had sensed the boat and sat silent, hidden in the rocks and trees along the steep bank of the little river. The boat carrying the High Priestess passed by, and while She sensed something, She could not cry out. It would have been foolish anyway, because unbeknownst to Her, there were weapons in the boat.

The soldiers took Her to the same old guard tower the Temple people had passed at the foot of the river; one that wasn't much used anymore. It sounded and smelled like the sea to Her there, reminding Her of Her home. When they pulled Her, none too gently, from the boat, She felt relieved. The entire way there, She had been in terror, not knowing if they had intended to throw Her into the river and drown Her. They half carried, half dragged Her to the stone tower, up some steps and into a stone room. They unbound Her there and locked Her in with no explanation of anything. In this room, there was nothing but a single bed with a straw mattress that smelled strongly of mildew. She was shivering and noticed a small open window with a cold wind off the sea; the kind that brings storms. She sat down on the bed and began to weep uncontrollably.

The door opened, and one of them, a Roman, came in, slapped Her, and told Her, "Answers when questions are asked of You is what we want to hear from You, nothing more."

This silenced Her, but pretty soon a noise slipped out of Her again. The door opened again. The guard came in and hit Her again. "Not off to a very good start, are You!" he said, pushing Her down on Her back on the bed.

Sometime later, one of them, Roman again, came in and tied Her to the bed on Her stomach. The strong smell of mold and mildew was repugnant to Her. She couldn't clear Her nose. A feeling of foreboding, dread and terror grew in Her until it became nearly unbearable. She made a little sound and a man came in and hit Her on Her back with what felt like a whip. She tried to use Temple practices to lift out of these feelings. Soon it was first light. Her heart yearned to see the Head of the Temple for Their morning practices at this time of day. Her heart was hurting Her so much She wanted to cry out again, but didn't dare.

She drifted out in meditation and was startled by the door opening again. This time, She was given a lash with a whip across Her backside. "Quite a fall for the High Priestess of the Great Temple at Delphi," he growled sarcastically. Without Her being able to see him, he began to ask Her just the kind of questions She did not want to have to answer. When she refused to answer, he said, "all right, have it your way," which was not Her way at all, and raped Her brutally, even cutting Her and sucking Her blood at the same time.

A little while later, She realized She needed to empty Her body wastes, but there was no opportunity for that. After a while, they just came out in the bed. She felt great shame and wanted to wash Herself, but there was no possibility of that. She was very thirsty, but they did not bring Her any water. She was hungry, but they brought Her no food. Instead, they watched Her through the closable opening She had seen in the door and insulted Her. Both in

Latin and in Greek, they used the worst slang of the times, the equivalent of some of it would have been, "The High Priestess stinks like a common soldier. Her piss stinks, too! Wonder what that would taste like? The nectar of the gods? Bitter? Sweet?" Someone said, "Sour! Does Your shit smell like the rest of us, too? We didn't think the High Priestess had to piss and shit like a common soldier, and if She did, we didn't think it would stink like a common soldier." She felt like a dog.

Later, they took Her for Her first interrogation. When She saw Her interrogator, She stiffened. He had had audiences with Her at the Temple. She felt he was the one who had raped Her, but She also felt suddenly unsure of Herself. He gave Her an invitation to talk to him about Greeks She knew who were on a list He handed to Her. When She remained silent, he said, "I thought You were going to learn to tell us what we want to know. It will go easier for You if you do. Talk to me about the Greeks on this list. I know You can tell me things about everyone of them."

Stinging tears were coming down Her face as She only glared at him. He called a man in who whipped Her in his presence with the kind of whip that has several knotted ends, then, he threw Her into a chair. As if nothing had happened, the interrogator said, "Talk to me. If You do not talk to me, it is only going to get worse."

"1 do not know anything I would tell you," She said then, "and You know it."

"You are being very, very foolish," he said. "You do not know how foolish You are being. You think You are protecting people, but Your silence tells me as much as if You were talking. Your hatred for Rome is well known and not well-founded. You are making too much of Yourself, as though You know when You do not know. You do not know the half of it. You do not even know who has been talking to us behind Your back. So much for the oracle who cannot be fooled! If You want to think You are protecting such people, You will pay for it, but they will not. They will only feel the pleasure of getting revenge for having been made to feel like You know better than they do when You do not. Now; let's start with this. Where is the Head of the Temple?"

After She had insisted for long enough, in spite of repeated slaps, that She did not know, he had Her returned to Her room. She had no choice but to attend to Her body needs on the floor of Her room. That night, Her interrogator came to Her room and raped Her in every orifice, cutting Her more, also, and sucking Her blood, which She felt all over Her body like a spreading sickness. He raped Her telling Her, "You are not going to refuse me! Now the anti goes up. Every time You do not comply, the anti goes up."

Later, She was taken to the interrogation room. Still, no water. When he began to question Her again, She said, "Please, may I have some water."

He went silently to the pitcher of water from which he was drinking freely in front of Her, poured some water in a vessel, and said, "Physical needs? I thought surely the High Priestess could rise above them," and threw it scornfully in Her face.

"I will not last much longer this way," She said to him.

"You don't tell me what's going to happen. I tell you. You are in no position to tell me anything. I give the orders, not You. You will last however long I decide you will last. You can't even die unless I decide to let you, and you can't live unless I let you! Remember that!"

The rest of the day and into the night She was questioned and beaten and brought to when She passed out until She didn't know where She was, what She was really saying yes to, what She was saying no to, or even who She was saying it to. She was so tired; so tired. Her heart felt so very heavy. If only She could just sleep, but whenever She started to slip away, Her interrogator had a way of bringing Her back. "Please," She begged, "Please, leave Me alone." Then She was afraid She had said that to the Head of the Temple and cried out the opposite, "Please, don't leave Me alone."

But, it was not the Head of the Temple. He was neither there, nor could He rescue Her. She did not know He was already dead of a heart attack on the way to the boat, and that She was seeing His energy field nearby. He could see what was going on and saw that if He spoke to Her it was likely to encourage Her to say things She should not say there. He was trying to lift Her out of Her body. My Light was also there, but whenever She got to the place where She might have been able to let go and come to One of Us, Her interrogator managed to pull Her back. Lucifer still had too much of a hold on Her. She was confused by the many voices there. "You're causing this Yourself. If You would have complied from the beginning, everything would have been much easier for You. We are trying to help You here, but You are not letting us. You are still stubbornly behaving as though You know best. Look at what thinking You know best has gotten You now. You deserve all of this and more."

THE MOVEMENT GOES UNDERGROUND

Late that night they took Her, hands still bound behind Her back, and marched Her down a stairway that wound around the inside of the outer wall of the tower until they were in the most subterranean chamber there. Her face was too swollen to see well, but She tried to note where She was, in some strange, self-distracting way, as though it made a difference anymore and as though She was still harboring some dim hopes of being physically rescued. Even if She could scream, which She dared not, She did not think it would be heard over the wind and sea by anyone from the outside "Getting free is not possible," they said to Her, as if they could read Her mind. "You'll never be free again."

As They descended, She was feeling vertigo. When Her swollen eyes got a glimpse of what they were taking Her to and what it looked like they intended to do to Her, Her legs went out from under Her. Her captors angrily ordered Her to get up, but She could not. The one who seemed to be the head of it pushed Her over the side of the stairs and let Her fall to the stone floor. She could not break Her fall, and Her shoulder was broken there. They took no notice.

They dragged Her to a stone slab, put Her on Her back and chained Her to rings on the sides. The chains were very heavy in case She became very strong in resistance to their torture as they had noticed others had, but She could not move. She was in too much pain.

Being told not to move seemed to bring alive, in stinging intensity, an itching that was screaming at her, not only from the wounds and vinegar on her back and many other places, but from everywhere that suddenly wanted to move. She began to twitch from the pain and the sudden itching on Her back. They commanded Her not to move and put the screws to Her head and hips. If She moved, they tightened the screws. They shaved off Her dark, wavy hair and burned it. Sniffing it as though it was incense to them, they made derisive comments about how horrible the High Priestess smelled. She felt both shamed and enraged.

Two others entered the room. She saw that one was deformed, seemed demented and possibly retarded. Her terror was shaking and shivering with cold. "What's the matter, can't You make Yourself warm with Your great powers?" one of them sneered.

Another one built a fire in a little raised fire pit next to Her. They began to heat some irons in the fire. "If the High Priestess is cold, hungry, or thirsty, we have to give Her something to drink, feed Her and warm Her up; whatever the High Priestess wants, we must be sure to do! We must serve the High Priestess…and after a pause…for dinner!" Then, they laughed.

One of them gave Her something to drink, but it was a potion of drugs to amplify everything and make Her talk. She could not stop shaking. "Look at Her! We don't have to do anything to gain Her favors; She's already lost control of Herself in desire for us!" another said.

"Let's screw Her! Let's screw Her now before She has an orgasm without us," the deformed one said.

The one in charge said, "Shut up and make Her stop! We have to clean Her up and improve Her first, She's not really good enough for us yet. First, I'm going to warm Her up."

He went to Her feet and used the irons to begin burning them on the bottoms. Fire shot up through Her meridians. When She realized they were burning Her feet, She made the judgment that even if She was rescued now, it was already too late. She was ruined and could never be healed again. She felt like there was no point in living without feet to walk on.

"Are you warm now? Are you warm now?" the demented one kept asking Her, drooling on Her and leering over Her.

She was dripping in cold sweat from the pain. If She recoiled or made a sound, they tightened the screws, cursed Her in Latin and in Greek and told Her the equivalent of, "Shut up and hold still."

The one burning Her feet began to ask Her questions. She cursed them all and began to rage, growling and gnashing Her teeth like a wild beast. The demented one and the other one began making sneering comments. "Mmmm, roast priestess for dinner," as he pulled off bits of her feet, making loud smacking noises as he ate them. "Spicy too! Give us some more slut!"

She shut Her eyes to not see it. It felt like the demented one had his penis in his hand already, and he did. She raged even more. The other one told Her to shut up and open Her eyes. She had sickening, burning pain shooting through Her entire body and voices screaming in pain in Her head. They "surgically" drilled a small hole in Her skull and pounded in a tube through which they could blow drugs directly into Her brain and alter Her consciousness in whatever ways they wanted. She felt that She was going to go absolutely crazy if She could not jump up and rescue Herself immediately, but remembered She was chained, and they were destroying Her feet. She raged at them, the equivalent in English of, "By the power of the gods, I curse you! Damn you to the worst echelons of hell!"

As they were chortling, they demanded She be silent. Then they laughed and said, "We're already in the worst echelons of Hell and we're going to bring You down here with us. Not so bad, is it?"

"Yes! It's terrible! Stop it right away!"

"It can get worse," the one burning Her feet said.

"We heard the High Priestess can handle anything. It doesn't matter about the gods. Your gods can't help You now. Who do You think is going to save You? There are no gods with the power to save You, and there are no gods with the power to damn us. If You have so much power, You make us stop!"

She closed her eyes in silent prayer. One of them said, "Open your eyes! Look at us! You do not see! You think others don't see what they need to see! You don't see what you need to see! You're going to look at everything you haven't wanted to see! We want you to see everything! We don't want you to be able to look away from anything."

They told Her they were going to make sure She looked at everything they did because they were going to cut Her eyelids off. This they did very slowly and precisely, commanding Her to hold still the entire time, tightening the screws if She even flinched when they cut or returned with the blade after wiping blood off of it. They did everything slowly and precisely, as though they were only doing medical experiments.

They gave Her some little time for the bleeding to stop which they helped with more salt water. "Oops," they said sometimes to deliberately frighten Her that She would be plunged into blindness next, but their slips were mostly deliberate, and they enjoyed increasing Her terror. The pain caused Her to pass out.

She didn't know if she was asleep or awake when She heard voices saying, "Where have Your gods gotten You? They've gotten You here. Did You think You were favored by the gods? If You were favored by the gods, they needed to save You before now. So much for how perfect and good and superior and smart You pretended to be! You're less favored than us; we have the power now!"

Then, the one at Her feet began breaking the bones in Her feet, one by one, very slowly and deliberately, stretching Her foot and making the tension unbearable before breaking the bones. With each bone he broke, he said something. "You deserve this and so much more. You have not helped anyone. You have made Yourself much too important. You have not listened to others the way You should have. You think You know what You are doing, but You do not. You think You are so right, but You are not. You think You are right to hate Romans, but You are not. You were supposed to be loving. What is the High Priestess doing hating anyone? The High Priestess is supposed to love everyone and help everyone who comes to Her, but You have not helped anyone and have hated everyone. You are no High Priestess and never should have been sitting in Her seat. You should not even be allowed to walk on the face of the Earth."

If She seemed to want to say something, the one in charge commanded Her again, "Be silent, unless we tell You to talk. Every time You are not silent, we are going to turn the screws."

She sank into wordless terror. Part of Her wanted to sob, but at the first hint of a sob, they tightened the screws. The cracking noises were as frightening to Her as the pain, and Her back was tightening in dread of each break. She tried to rise above it, but he was watching Her very closely and seemed to know when to break the bone. Crying out helped Her pain, but they would not let Her. If She flinched when he broke a bone, the others tightened the screws. They noticed that She was arching Her back when they inflicted pain. One of them got over Her. Screaming, "Lie still!" He slammed Her pelvis down onto the stone slab with such force that he broke it.

One of them began to pound Her relentlessly with questions again about everything they thought She might know, including the power and magic of the Temple, about its rituals, its wealth and even about its library. She couldn't think. When She didn't want to talk, even about the library, one of them said, "Surely there is no problem telling us about the library. I'm sure You would like Romans to read these things and learn to think the way You do."

She began to mumble and stumble over Her words. "No! No!" she screamed, "Stop! Stop!"

"Silence! You cannot stop us. There is no stopping us," One replied. The demented one tightened the screws. "You have no power as High Priestess anymore. You had no real power anyway, only what was given to You. You have been thrown down from Your high position, and no one cares! We can do anything we want with You, and no one cares! You have no value to Yourself or others unless You talk to us and tell us what we want to hear,"

As much as by the physical pain and knowing it was going to get much, much worse, she was horrified by the heartlessness. Heartlessness to Her meant no limits to the cruelty, and that struck terror into Her heart. The one at Her feet said, "Why were You so silly as to try to help people who don't care about You? You think You have power in the world? You do not! You are ours now, but then, You were always ours, and so, we can do whatever we want with You. We're going to have as much fun as we can with You and then throw You away!"

They all affirmed this loudly and enthusiastically with grunts and roars, shrieks and hideous laughter, accompanied by every sort of social grossness; spitting, drooling, stomping, farting, belching, urinating, humping motions stirring up the dogs that were there and carrying on as though it was a big party, and to them, it was. "We can screw You and we can eat You if we want to, and we will," they told Her, and all the while, the demented one seemed to take delight in repeating, over and over, certain phrases that seemed to be the most key ones for penetrating deeply into Her subconscious.

She screamed at them, "You cannot do these horrible things to Me and make Me be silent! You cannot give Me this horrible pain and tell Me I cannot make any sound. Have you no feelings? How can you be so heartless? I hate you! You are not even human!" She was screeching and screaming in rage, and like all the beasts of hell, it came reverberating back into her ears; barking, hissing, growling, hooting and howling with derisive laughter along with the repetitious reciting of, "You're the one who is not human. You say we're heartless, but You are the one who is screaming in hatred here. You are the One who needs to look at who is heartless here!"

The one at Her feet said coldly, "We have plenty of feelings, and one of them is feelings of hatred toward a woman who has not learned Her place."

Incensed, She made more sounds of rage and growled, "You are just like all the Romans who want to overrun people and not care what they think or feel about it! You don't see what you are really doing! Why don't you see what you are doing? Because you are all stupid and hateful ogres and boars! You don't see what I was trying to do. You don't see anything. You are just stupid!"

The one she could not see said, "Oh? Is there no one like that in Delphi?"

"No!" she said.

"Oh, really, are you sure of that? What about the head of your City State? Hasn't he been stupid?"

She felt Her anger at him, "Yes!" she said. "Stupid, stupid, stupid," she continued saying to Herself in Her great anger at it all.

He asked Her about others, then, and got quite a bit of the information he wanted to be able to see who would help Rome take over Greece. The others were laughing while this was going on, and the demented one was saying, "The High Priestess is going to enlighten us by telling us how stupid we are!

The one questioning Her said, "You can't enlighten stupid people; You should know that already! You are the One who is stupid! That is why we are here and You are there!"

The pain and drugs had put Her in places She did not understand. Someone else joined them there. The High Priestess sensed this, but hallucinated it was someone from the Temple. She began to talk to him as though She was talking to him about an advanced class She was teaching.

They were delighted. He began to ask some questions, but some of them let Her know he was not who She thought he was, and something in Her knew not to say certain things. She talked for a while. When She stopped talking, one of them sneered, "This is the great High Priestess who knows everything and was going to save Greece! She thought She was going to save the world! You cannot save the world! We're all too stupid! How stupid of You to have squandered Yourself to save people You do not care about because they're all too stupid. You are not going to save anything! You can't even save Yourself! If You're so all knowing, what good has it done You!?"

The High Priestess started growling again. "Be silent, woman! You never learned Your place! The Head of the Temple must not have been much of a man if he let You behave like this there!"

"You wouldn't know!" She growled. "It doesn't matter. He's gone."

"Oh, where?" Her interrogator said.

"I don't know," She said. They tightened the screws so much She did not think She could endure it without Her head bursting open. She began rolling Her body back and forth on the stone slab. This wracked Her broken bones, but She hardly noticed it compared to the pain they were inflicting now. "Where is he?" he demanded.

She passed out and was jolted awake by pain and, then, instant fear of what they were doing to Her now. They were burning out one of Her eardrums saying She must not be answering because She couldn't hear, so they were fixing it so She could hear better.

"I don't know!" She screamed and screamed and screamed.

"Silence," one of them commanded, "or You're going to force us to cut out Your tongue!"

"Stupid! Stupid! Stupid! She's stupid, stupid, stupid!" the demented one kept repeating as they made plans to cut Her tongue out and discussed all of the grisly ways they could do it, from dropping it down Her throat and suffocating Her to drowning Her in all the blood to giving Her little pieces at a time and making Her swallow them. "No! I want to eat Her tongue!" another one said.

"They're all good! Let's do all of it!" the demented one said to every new idea. "Let's go down Her throat now and cut her tongue out later," another said. "Why wait to have fun!" Her terror made Her grow silent.

"Now, You're going to learn what Your mouth is for!" one said. She wasn't allowed to answer. She could not answer, because they were forcing Her mouth open and sticking their fingers in there like they were going to pull Her teeth. "Not yet," one of them said. Let's see if She bites us first."

She tried to bite them then, and they told Her it was a wrong idea because She had just made it worse for Herself. They pulled out Her front teeth, one by one, and dropped them down Her throat. Then, they began raping Her down Her throat, deeply raping Her; pounding Her with objects in Her other orifices and doing other things She could not keep track of in the desperate nausea and gagging, suffocation terror. She could still hear them screaming at Her, "If you know so much, why can't You save Yourself? Where are all of Your powers now? You have no right to question us! You have no right to tell us what to do! You don't know anything we need to know. We don't need to be told what to do! Who are You to tell us what to do? Everything has already been decided by more important people than You! If You and Your gods know so much, where are Your gods now? Your gods can't help You now, because You don't receive the gods. You don't listen to anybody. You think You know better than the gods. You're a fake! Rome has gods that are more powerful than Greece. Your gods have failed You, or Rome could not take over Greece. The Roman gods do not like the Greek gods."

Just when She felt She was nearly dead from suffocation, they let off because they didn't want to kill Her yet. She had to gasp for air there, gagging back Her vomit, and as soon as they thought She had enough air, another raped Her down the throat. When they finished, She was not conscious, but not quite dead. They threw water on Her to revive Her, and She came to thinking they were drowning Her. She did not dare make any sound. She did not move, either. She was cowered in terror now. She hardly breathed, hoping they would not notice that She had come to, but that was not much comfort because She realized they were still doing things. They threw salt water on Her feet, and She jerked Her feet without realizing She had done it.

"She's not learning!" one of them said. They angrily unchained her. She could not stand, but they dragged Her to the rack. She saw a big snake moving on the floor. He looked like the python from the Temple, and lifted his head threateningly toward Her. They laid Her on the rack and began stretching Her, giving Her fits of pain. She began a growling rage from between gritted teeth that grew in intensity the more they stretched Her on the rack, until She was raging like a wild animal and was making so much noise they had the thought that She might think She had the power to break loose from the rack. They told Her again that She had no power and commanded Her to be silent, but She could not hear them.

When they did not stop Her rage with their commands, they began drowning and suffocating Her with wet rags. "Who's the beast?" they growled at Her in their fury. "You're every bit as much a beast as everyone else, and don't forget it!"

She was drowning, and they knew just when to stop and let Her come back so they could do it again. They sent Her down into a terror that had no trust and seemed to have no end to its increasing intensity, or any bottom to it, until She passed out only for as long as they let Her.

We tried to get Her then, but She had too much self-hatred and shame and too many judgments against Herself to let go or even to know if letting go would take Her to unloving light or Loving Light or into the original darkness again. She was very terrified and confused, as She had been for a long time. She was experiencing both My Light and the Father of Manifestation as just out of reach, and the torturers had been stopping their suffocation and drowning of Her just before She died. They knew just how much to let Her breathe that was not enough to get over the exhaustion of Her struggle and then drown Her again, overwhelming Her strength and exhausting Her further into the terror that She could not even escape by dying.

Among other things, they were telling Her She was a fool to fight for Her life, had nothing to live for, if She had just learned to obey Her superiors She wouldn't be in this position, if She would just give up and let go, She could die and get it over with, and then, bring Her back just before She could die, telling Her She could not even die unless they decided to allow it. They also told Her She could not let go and die because She had to control everything so much that She could not even let go and die, and that they were only trying to help Her by teaching Her how to surrender and let go, even to death.

Over and over, they did this, sometimes pouring some water down Her throat so that She felt She had no power to keep this out of Her body. In moments of consciousness during this, She could hear the one She feared was the most demented, because they all looked this way to Her now, repeating over and over, "Yeah, beasts, we're all beasts. You're a beast, too, little girlie, don't forget that!"

This was punctuated by bouts of hateful laughter. In another moment of consciousness, She saw him standing in the midst of the dogs, exciting himself and them sexually. Moving into Her field of vision again, as though they were all in a strobe lighting situation, She saw him having sex with one of the dogs in a frenzy, while the other dogs there were barking and jumping around him and jerking as though they were ejaculating, too. When She tried to focus for an instant to see if She was really seeing this, She could not see anything with Her physical eyes and feared She was becoming as demented as they were. When pain from the rack jerked Her body there, they said, "Look, she's jerking, too! She likes it! Do it some more. She has been hiding this from us! She's orgasming here, too! She's having secret orgasms."

She was too weak to do anything but try to gain some air that Her body was desperately driving Her for, although She could not understand why Her body would continue to struggle for life there.

"She's been withholding Her response from us, but now She has to give it to us!" one of them said. She shuddered, and they called that an orgasm, too, tormenting Her with more comments to which She could not respond. "Look, She likes it! Do it some more! She wants it! She's just pretending She doesn't! Let's give Her some!"

She was babbling to the previous Head of the Temple as though he was there, begging him to help Her, rescue Her and heal Her. I felt it was My Light She was talking to. "No one is ever rescued! Unless You really have magic powers, You can't rescue Yourself, either! If You have magic powers, where are they? You waited too long to rescue Yourself; You're too far gone now!" The torturers said.

She continued to babble as though it was true. Then, they decided to play along with this and see what would happen. In Her babbling, she was mumbling all sorts of things. They already had plans of their own, but, took some cues from Her to cruelly play with Her. They took Her off the rack and carried Her back to the stone slab. She was limp. "If he's real, why doesn't he come get you now?" to which she had no reply. They went on, "He must want You to suffer; he must want You to pay a lot and sacrifice Yourself here. He must be empowering us to do this, or he would have carried You away already. He must not be as powerful even as Roman chains," laughing coarsely at their own cleverness and Her presumed hallucinations.

They were saying these things while She was limp there, while at the same time doing some internal work on Her genitals. "She doesn't think She looks good, but She doesn't know what he really wants. That's why She isn't good enough. If She's going to be rescued now, let's improve Her for him first. They threw some water on Her. "We're cleaning You up so You'll look nice when You get rescued." "Oh, thank you," She said. They rolled their eyes at each other.

"Oh, My hair, My beautiful hair is gone."

Then, they said, "Wait! She's not ready yet. She doesn't like Her hair anymore. Let's fix Her hair for him, too. We don't want Her to feel like She's not looking good if She's going to be rescued. Let's fix Her up. Let's make Her even better than She was. Let's improve Her so he'll want Her even more. We know what he wants. Let's make Her even more attractive."

They began to pound little nails into Her skull. "We're giving You a new hairdo," they told Her. She screamed in pain. "Stop screaming. Your rescuer doesn't like screaming." When that didn't silence Her, they threatened to suffocate Her some more. They gave Her an extra snort of drugs through the little tube and said, "You're all ready for him now."

Suddenly, there was a wind that came into the room, as though a great doorway had been opened, and they told Her it must be true, She was going to be rescued after all. They put out all the light sources except the fire by Her side, as though the wind had done it, and acted like they were being blown back by the wind, too. They told Her they were all afraid of this power, and the one who could do that must be the one who was going to rescue Her.

We did not want to abandon Her there, but feeling how Our presence so close to Her seemed to be confusing Her more than it was helping and prolonging Her ability to stay alive in this. We did not want that or to have Her imprint that Our presence meant We approved of what was happening to Her there. We decided to pull back until She seemed more ready to leave Her body there. When We pulled back, this also gave Her many problems and confusions. Not only was She not rescued, now She had a dark silence around Her in which She felt very terrified and abandoned again, but She was losing some consciousness now and might have to suffer less because of it.

Her subconscious was experiencing all of it vividly, though, and the drugs were making it much worse than it would have been otherwise, vivifying all of the sensory perceptions and opening Her subconscious mind to them. I foresaw a problem lifting Her out of Her body because She was feeling so sure that She was going to the darkness forever. I wanted Body to get a hold of Her before She went down too far, but Body was so angry with Her for letting this happen that he let Her go down too far before he helped My Light lift Her up. I couldn't lift Her very far toward Me. I thought She was resistant, and Her shame was as though She was in the plane of reversal again, but that wasn't all there was to it. I hadn't realized, yet, that Body was preventing it by holding Her too firmly in an angry grasp that imprinted Her that this was My Light's feeling toward Her.

THE CONCLUSION OF THE HIGH PRIESTESS'S LIFE AT DELPHI

The High Priestess's mind was barely functioning by now, and She sank into the many imprints She had originally formed about the light without being able to comprehend what they were. These imprints were receiving an intense recharge in Her subconscious. Some of these imprinted judgments were that the light was cold, unfeeling and uncaring, that the light only cared about what it wanted, that the light could do anything to Her because it didn't feel or care, that the light would go to any lengths to prevail, that the light abandoned Her whenever She really needed it, that the light broke Her heart because She so wanted to have a loving companion and received hatred instead, that the light didn't love or care about Her or Her experience, that the light never was and never would be willing to or capable of helping Her or rescuing Her from anything, that She'd been fooled by Her own perceptions and that the light set Her up to be played for a fool. She was going into bitterness, and while I couldn't blame Her, I couldn't help Her, either.

She was lying there in all of this while they were having a discussion as though what She had experienced already was no problem. She still screamed sometimes and mumbled things that infuriated them. They thought they had already gotten as much information out of Her as they could, and of all the horrible things they discussed they could do, and wanted to do, they decided that now they were going to cut out Her tongue.

She's still lippy," one of them said. "She hasn't learned Her place. We have to cut out Her tongue," another said. "She's asked for it." One of them grabbed Her tongue with hot tongs that burned right through what they gripped and cut off the front part of Her tongue. They roasted it and ate it. "You cannot bother us by speaking now," they told Her, "so forever hold Your peace!"

Then, they took out Her tonsils, gave them to the dogs, and cauterized Her throat and Her gums. When She made gurgling, gagging noises, they started breaking Her fingers, one by one. "More like a real vagina now," the deformed one said.

She could not swallow, and feared swallowing what was left of Her tongue. They raped Her in the mouth again. Over and over, they came, one by one, until She did not know how many of them there were. There was almost nothing left of Her then, and several times, I thought surely She would die there, especially because of the dry heaves and suffocation they were causing with their pounding penises. They complained about how dull it was to rape the great High Priestess because She was so sexless and wouldn't give them what they wanted. They began a brutal, pounding raping of Her with phallic type objects. With each round of it, they would insert a larger phallic type of object, screaming at Her, "Is this enough? Is this enough? What does it take to get a High Priestess to lose control of Herself in orgasm?"

They didn't know what was keeping Her alive for so long. They were openly congratulating themselves on their skill and telling Her She was still alive because of their good care. Torture victims were better than cadavers to some Roman doctors because they were living flesh, and they could see how living flesh reacted. There was a Roman doctor there who was learning as much as he could from this. He took great pride in his precision work, and often ejaculated more strongly than if he was having intercourse.

We're going to feed you, so you don't starve to death," one of them told Her.

"To yourself !" the deformed one cackled.

They were going to peel the skin off Her arms. As they peeled the skin off with more slow, cold, precision, the pain was excruciating. She did not know how She could possibly be living through all of this and was fearing that She really could not die unless they let Her.

"We're not going to let you die," they told Her. "We're having too much fun!"

As can so often happen with the reflections of denial spirits, it was as if they knew Her in great detail. They told Her that as such a high, spiritual priestess, She should not have to breath through Her nose and mouth. She had not been able to attain a state of breathlessness like some had done in the Temple. This had fed Her feelings of self-hatred and doubt, but their method had denied even more terror into Her, and She did not know it. When people heard about the state of breathlessness, many thought that to not breath through the nose and mouth meant they must be breathing through their skin. The torturers told Her they were helping Her to breath through Her skin since Her suffocating hadn't shown them that She could. They put alum on Her arms and while they were doing it, they put some more in Her mouth. "Water," She mumbled then.

"Yes, of course, Your most High Priestess!" Then the demented, retarded and deformed one urinated into Her mouth. When She tried to shut Her mouth, another forced it open. She was forced to swallow it.

"See, She likes it. She just doesn't let Herself know what She really likes! Let's give Her some more! We want to give Her what She wants, whether She pretends She doesn't like it or not!" They all urinated on Her then.

The drugs they gave Her were not anesthetics. They had been taking drugs that had various psychedelic effects, and She soon found Herself plunged into another hell of strange visions, distorted sounds and amplified feelings. It did not seem like long to Her before She was assailed by noxious smells. It seemed to Her that they were putting things into the fire that smelled terrible. It was pieces of skin, hair, bones and shit. She felt like She was going to throw up, but dared not. "Just cleaning up after You," they said, laughing horribly at Her and smacking their lips as they ate some of it. "You are so gross, like a sow who can't clean up after Herself. You think we're repulsive. You're repulsive," they told Her.

They put some roasted pieces of Her own skin into Her mouth. When Her face grimaced, they told Her, "You're in no position to be picky about what You eat. Then they began to do some surgical operations on Her, and even though She passed out from pain exhaustion, they awakened Her again with their drugs for Her to find that they had put pieces of Her liver and other parts of Her body in Her mouth. They removed Her gall bladder and poured bile down Her throat. They removed most of Her right breast, toasted it and ate it right in front of Her, giving Her small pieces and commanding Her to swallow them.

They rested during Her "little break," as they called it. Next, they decided to cut off Her leg. They roasted it, ate of it and tossed the rest to the dogs. When the dogs had gnawed it clean to their satisfaction, they took it back. Still insulting Her as the cause of how sexually dissatisfied they were, they got on top of Her and began going down Her throat again with another one battering up from Her vagina with Her leg bone. They were, literally, pounding Her from both ends, which gave them more satisfaction raping Her down Her throat until they spasmed in some kind of drug-driven ejaculation, stumbled off of Her, still jerking like the dogs, stumbling around the room like madmen until they collapsed on the floor and lay where they fell. They lay there in a stupor and fell into a sleep that lasted quite a while. They gave Her a little "rest" then, but really it was a rest for them.

Still, She could not come to Us, and We did not know why. I felt so horrified by all of this that I could hardly even look at it, but I knew I had to. They began to come to and decided they weren't finished yet. They stomped on Her, they urinated on Her, they defecated on Her and smeared it all over Her. They twisted Her neck until it broke. They pulverized Her in every way they could think of until there was no way to recognize Her and almost no way to tell She was even a human. While they were doing this, they were screaming at Her, "Go ahead and die, because now, we want You to! We never want to have to see You again!"

They slammed Her pelvis against the stone slab She was on, breaking where Her pelvis joined Her spine, then, Her spine in many places as the fury of their pounding and their slams increased. She was unconscious. She was bleeding from all of Her orifices, and the demented one was licking it up, as were the dogs that were jumping on top of Her now, too. Still not satisfied, they melted some lead, telling Her that She was a big, gaping, dark hole that no one could satisfy. As soon as the lead was molten enough, they boosted Her pelvis up, broken bones and all, and poured it in. It overflowed and burned the entire area. Even though they did not know She had any consciousness left, She screamed in agony and went unconscious. As soon as the lead was cool enough, they unchained Her and shoved Her onto the floor.

The dogs began to tear at Her. The snake seemed to take his time gliding over to Her, swallowing discarded lumps of whatever on the way. The snake cruised the length of Her body, and then, ignoring the dogs, wrapped himself around Her entire body and began to squeeze. As the snake squeezed, She let out a powerful and prolonged scream which did not seem to be at all humanly possible. It scared Her torturers so much they almost bolted from the room. The snake continued to squeeze until the scream subsided and then bit Her in Her third eye, as he had always wanted to do.

A few days later, they threw the High Priestess's mangled body down on the steps of the Temple. The High Priestess and the rest of the Temple people who had fled, had already been heavily discredited in the eyes of the people by Roman infiltrators. The Romans wanted the Temple's power, reputation and influence reduced, and they had succeeded in ruining it. Horrifying as it was to gaze upon the remains of Her body, by then, many of the people stared blankly, not appearing to be disturbed by Her fate. They had been made afraid of Her and of the Temple, and now feared that the Temple had been controlling all of Delphi and their lives in ways they had not known.

I took note of this, and learned something about fragmentation, or the common people, as they are usually called, so often not seen as useful or as having any opinions that matter until their opinions are needed by those who have manipulated them to serve the dark purposes hidden there. When the High Priestess's body was thrown down there, the Head of the City State said that whatever Her powers were, they were not the right and good powers to have, or She would have been more favored by the gods, and She could not, then, have come to this end. The crowds assembled there gave a cry of outrage to which was said, "We are mere mortals, the tools of the gods. This could not have happened if it was not meant to happen because the gods wanted it this way."

All of the things that were wrong were quickly cited. No attempt was encouraged, or even allowed, to look any deeper to see what was right and what was wrong. When some came forward in defense of the Temple and the Seers, they were told, "Hit or miss! If you say enough things, some of them are going to be right."

THE ISLE

There were many emotions in the people leaving the Temple that night. Not only the feeling of not knowing where they were going, and of quite possibly leaving their family, friends and homeland forever, but also of feeling they may be in great peril, not only behind them, but also in front of them. There was a great wind as though the gods were angry. Some said it was because the gods wanted to make sure they could not be followed by sea, some said that the gods were angry because the High Priestess had caused the Temple to lose favor with the gods, some said that it was the High Priestess trying to strike them down and some said it was the Romans trying to stop them from leaving.

Other points of view among them said it was their fate to stay and that they should go back and face whatever fate awaited them there. Others said it was the Roman gods fighting with the Greek gods. All of this was mental conjecture to avoid feeling their feelings. What the people of the Temple, themselves, were not letting themselves feel or move emotionally was not even considered as to why the sea was stormy when they wanted to leave.

The man who put himself forward as the one who should lead them now that the Head of the Temple was gone, is the one who took in the High Priest's denied rage. He began to speak to them in definite tones that sounded like the High Priest, Himself, especially on His last day when He was getting them together to leave. They did not notice it, at first, as anything other than using the tone the previous Head of the Temple had used, and it allayed their fears to be told what to do. They liked it that this man was taking charge now and even taking on some of the former Head of the Temple's physical mannerisms to a startling degree, and rather suddenly, right when they most needed someone to help them. I noticed it as a vivid example of how denials can leave the person making them and go into another person. When I saw the Father of Manifestation let the Mother go too far down before He agreed with My Light that We had to lift Her, I also knew that denials can have many layers to them.

The one taking charge of leading them now was very definite about having to leave as though he had some sort of inner knowing and everyone else decided to go with him. Now, they had to come down off the hillside and find the boatman. They didn't know where to look or who to look for. In their internal insistence that the Head of the Temple could not be leaving them when he was dying on the trail, only a few of them had even found out what name to ask for. They decided they should not all go into the fishing village at once, but the storm was making them feel that they must seek shelter. The man leading them now did not tell them that he had gotten the man's name from the High Priest. He said he thought he could find the way to the boatman, and the young woman said she would go with him to see what she could see about it.

The man this denied rage had configured around was a part of Heart who did not want to be seen as anything less than the Father, thought he knew better than the Father and didn't mind taking in this essence because he had plenty of rage, himself that was already polarized to the Head of the Temple's point of view. He experienced this only as though he had suddenly come into his own or as though the torch had been passed to him, and he was proud to take it. He believed he could succeed here, not only because he was smart, ready and qualified, but also because he had listened closely to the Head of the Temple before he died and had gathered more details than the others. Since this man had originally been from near this village, he thought he might even know the boatman. He and the young woman were able to find the boatman rather quickly in the village, but the boatman did not want to sail on such a night. They told him the others needed shelter from the impending storm. The boatman said the only place to shelter them was in the hull of the boat.

The boatman was Captain of his own little ship. He led these two to the boat. The young woman went to get the others, leading them to the boat in small groups. The man who was taking charge of them now stayed with the boatman. He did not want to tell this man that they were fleeing, but he knew they had to leave. He told the Captain that he must sail them down the coast, at least to the next fishing village, so that they could be sure that this boat was going to work out for them while they were still near enough to land to find another boat if they didn't like this one for any reason.

Desire for the gold he had been offered caused the Captain to say he would sail them enough to know that this boat was a worthy vessel for their trip. The man who had taken charge of leading the Temple people for this trip wasn't sure if he trusted this man because he had seen that there weren't enough provisions on the boat for the distance they wanted to go. He didn't know the Head of the Temple had had the Captain told to put on provisions for only a few days so as not to attract attention. He told the Captain they would have to see that for themselves.

When all the people were loaded, the man taking charge asked the Captain to now sail them at least to the next village. The Captain started to refuse and say that they had to wait out the storm. The man told him there were other boats, and if they had to do that, they might look around for other boats when the storm was over. He also told the boatman that he knew how to sail and that it wouldn't be that difficult to get to the next village if they left right away. The Captain agreed to try it if this man would help him sail the boat.

Hugging the coast as closely as they dared, they sailed to the next village. When they got there, there was no light. Storm winds soon began to assail the ship, and the Captain said he wanted to put in at the village. He had a foreboding feeling that the storm coming in was not typical of the season. With the winds came an excitement in the rage-polarized women. Their first thought was that it was the vengeance of the High Priestess because the Head of the Temple had taken Her gold Cobra belt. They soon decided, however, that without Her belt, She had no real power anymore, and began to say they were having visions that this had all happened because it was meant to happen, and that they were meant to be the new Temple. The Temple man said that if they must wait out the storm, he wanted to sail to the leeward side of an island to the south and wait out the storm there. The women told the Captain that they felt sure they had the protection of the gods. The Captain said it was bad luck to have women on board and asked the women to stay below deck.

Below deck was close quarters, dark and very turbulent. Some of the women began to feel seasick, but soon, their rage overcame these 'simple body sensations,' as they called them. They began trying on the High Priestess's belt. The young woman said she must try it on first. As the winds worsened, the women decided they must control the storm, which they had now decided was being sent by the gods to give them the escape they needed. Soon they were saying that they had called the storm, and began commanding the storm to drive them quickly on their way and to make pursuit impossible. Not allowed up top anymore, the Temple women, and some of the men, too, were shouting commands to the storm, but it was barely audible over the sounds of the weather all around them. Above them, on the deck, the Captain, the man who had taken the position of leadership with the Temple people and the Captain's small crew were fighting with lashing winds and driving rains, trying to keep the ship from capsizing.

The Temple man came below deck and found the other Temple people arguing about how they wanted the new Temple to be as though there was no problem from the storm. He told the women that the Captain was going to insist that the women be put off the boat and that he had no objection to that if they did not get their rage under control. When they told him they could not be put off the ship because the ship could not even get to a port, he told them that if they did not look at what was really happening to the ship, they were quite possibly going to end their lives by insisting they had to have this storm.

He insisted they calm down enough to realize what was really happening to the ship. When they did not listen to him, he asked the men to meditate together to calm the storm. When the women had no one to engage with them in this anymore, they began to feel that maybe he was right. They would not admit it, but they joined in the meditation, too, and asked the gods for safe and speedy delivery to their destination. The storm calmed, but the winds still remained rather high and gusty.

When the storm calmed, the man leading them felt he had had the power to do this more than anyone else on board and said that he should be the new Head of the Temple because the gods had favored him. Most of the other men said that was right. The young woman said that she wanted to have the position of High Priestess. The man who felt he should be the new Head of the Temple said he wanted to wait until they got to their destination and see how it felt then.

The women were feeling themselves to be goddesses and were seeing the men as judging against them and their power. They wanted a chance to try things their way, and being rage-polarized daughter and mother pieces, they thought they knew better than everyone else. All the women were fighting about who the new High Priestess should be and did not want to let the men have a say in that. The young woman was the most insistent on wearing the belt. Even though she had not been initiated or appointed, she said the former Head of the Temple had given it to her, which was not true. She saw where he had put it when he was readying them to leave and had gone into his things and taken it when he died on the trail. She claimed to be the best seer and said it was she who had had the clearest vision of where the boat was, and that without her, they probably wouldn't be on it yet.

The men were saying they had helped more than the women acknowledged and that they did not feel accepted by the women as a part of the inner circle of seers. They said that seeing was not just a feminine thing and that they were not just Temple scribes; they were healers and seers, too. The girl was adamant that she had to be the new High Priestess and that since there was no one to appoint her, she was going to appoint herself. The Heart man who felt he was the one who was really insuring the success of their journey, then stepped forward and said that he thought this must happen by consensus. That sounded reasonable to everyone but the young woman, who looked at him and said that the women didn't want him as the new Head of the Temple. They wanted another person who was with them, an older, more fatherly man.

This quieted the younger man who wanted to be their leader. Before any of the women could raise a voice of opposition to her statement, she said, with a "match this one" look in her eyes, that the women wanted to have the new Temple be their way most of the time, but she was sure none of the women would mind if the men got to have it their way some of the time. Then, without asking the other women, she said the men got to have their way on the four days of the year that would still be major ceremonies dedicated to the Sun; the solstices and the equinoxes. She waited until it looked like the men did not like this offer much and then said that on those four days, the men could do anything they wanted to do, including anything they wanted to do sexually, especially if the Moon was full, including having as many sexual partners as they wanted to have on those days.

The women all shrieked 'no' from their sexual shame, embarrassment, feelings this wasn't right and fear that no one would choose them, but when the men really liked the idea, the women gave in rather easily in exchange for having it their way most of the time. The young woman who wanted to be High Priestess was being stirred with old buried memories of Pangea, and their journey felt to her like an opportunity to have the experience of Pangea all over again. She had been describing her visions of the place they were going, and the more she described seeing this place as soft and lush, green and golden, the more others were also beginning to be stirred into old feelings of Pangea. They did not remember, then, where these feelings were coming from or details of Pan, but they knew something deep was stirring in them. Most of them, openly or secretly, wanted to have sex, and they wanted to lay their fears aside by telling themselves that it would be alright to have sex that way because it would all be part of rituals dedicated to the god of their original Temple, Apollo the Sun god.

Later, some splits began to appear in the men, and some of the women. The older man, who was Spirit-polarized, didn't want the position of Head of the Temple. He and the other Spirit-polarized men didn't want having sex to be a part of the Temple at all, while the men polarized more to Body did. Since the young woman had been secretly having sex with the Head of the Temple, and had had sex before with someone in the Temple, she assumed that everyone did or wanted to have sex. She decided to call them on it. She knew a little from things she had seen and been told and openly confronted them about having sex secretly. If they didn't admit it, she pressured them more by telling them she had seen that they had. They all decided, then, to leave it alone until they got to where they were going and see how they felt about it then, but, they were all titillated by Purple fantasies of sex and had fastened onto the word "anything."

After that, sexual tensions and excitements rose, because they all had secret desires for people in the Temple that had not been fulfilled at Delphi, and the Spring Equinox was not that far away. They did not know just what day they would arrive and were not sure anymore just what day it was at sea, but if all went well, it seemed they would make it to their destination just in time. It looked like it was going to be a full or bursting Moon, too, and they could have a grand ceremony to celebrate their arrival at the same time.

The Captain of the ship did not like any of these goings-on, and now that the weather had calmed, wanted to put them all off the boat at the nearest port; go back to Greece and say he had been on a fishing expedition. The women could not resolve this with him because he would not talk to the women, and the man who wanted to be Head of the Temple felt he had to give the Captain, and the crew, too, some more gold to induce them to keep going with them.

The Temple man had some fear that since they had so much gold with them that the Captain and his crew might decide to hold them captive in the hull, rob them right there on the ship and still put them off, or even try to throw them overboard one by one because of being so angry with them. He told the Temple people to pretend they did not have anything more, but the rage-polarized daughters did not listen to him. They continued to try on the High Priestess's gold cobra belt and let it be seen by a crew member who came below deck to check on them. This man had been to the Temple and knew what he was seeing when he saw the belt.

They sailed through Gibraltar smoothly and easily and in fair weather, just as the young woman had said they would. They were not stopped, and, since the Temple people were all below deck, they did not know that it was noticed how low their boat was riding in the water. Some of those observers were pirates and one of them also talked to Rome. The Captain, who was a seasoned sailor, felt uneasy now, as though he knew they had drawn attention to themselves, and the man who felt he was the leader of the group felt this way also. He began to think they should get another boat as soon as they could. He did not necessarily want to let this man go back to Greece in case he was going to be questioned, but he also did not want this man to know where they had gone. The Captain didn't know what might await him when he returned home, and the Temple man did not want to tell him. The Captain feared pirates if they left the Mediterranean. The Temple man decided to let the Captain take them to a nearby port for more provisions where he planned to look for another boat.

The would-be Head of the Temple found another, larger boat. That night, the women all got off the boat to walk around on land while the crew of the next boat loaded, and the Temple men transferred their possessions. Everyone was on the boat by dawn, and they sailed on, seemingly without incident, feeling that this all meant they were on the right path. They were feeling celebratory that things were going along so smoothly for them.

The young woman began to claim that she had begun to hear a Supreme God who had power over all the other gods. Saying she had been hearing Him all along, but didn't want to say it, she said that this made her the last word in the Temple. Others in the Temple did not like her attitude. They saw it as self-righteous and began having feelings of almost wishing something would upset her self-righteous confidence. Then, pirates struck; Viking pirates.

The Captain of their new boat said it was a bad sign and that they should go back to port. The Temple people did not want to live so close to Greece. They asked him to try to outrun them, but they could not and had to turn sharp starboard and sail into the fog the Captain had been trying to skirt. They had to be very quiet and pulled down most of their sails in hopes the pirates would not come upon them. They were drifting, and the Captain said they had a new peril now...rocky coastline. They waited, but the mists did not clear, and the Captain felt they were being strangely pulled. He thought it must be a current that was carrying them somewhere, and he did not know where. He was fuming mad.

The Heart man was holding his own rage back in a feeling that he needed to guide the situation. He told the Captain that he understood how he felt and that they would all disembark into his ferry boat and find the shore themselves so he could go his own way. They tried dropping anchor, but it was not shallow enough for that. The Temple people tried meditating, but there was no lift in the fog. It was clear the Captain wanted to get these Temple people off his boat. Several of the men felt sure that in a smaller boat they could row and, with someone at the helm, could find the shore. They did not understand that the swells could carry them onto rocks as easily as land them on a beach. The Captain said, "No."

At last they caught a glimpse of land, and the Captain agreed to let them go because it was not safe for him to get any closer. It was treacherous for them just to get the ferry boat so loaded with all of them and everything they could put in it. They set out, and with the help of the Heart man and all of their psychic perceptions, they were able to avoid the rocks, but found they were in a marshy area. They weren't finding any dry land there. At times, they thought they saw some dry land, but when they tried to ferry themselves to it, they either couldn't find it or found it was marshy. They felt like they were circling, apparently lost in the mists and marshland of what looked like such a dismal place to them that they felt unsure as to whether this really was their destination. They finally found a little place of drier land, but not knowing if there was any more, they did not want to unload. At least they could rest, but in the morning they still could not find any more dry land.

Faeries were doing all of this to them and studied them all night long without the Temple people knowing it, other than having perceptions of being watched and wondering if they were going to be attacked by local people they had not seen yet. The Faeries were both fascinated and made uneasy by the Temple people because they had not seen light like theirs for a long time. They wanted the mists to lie upon the land until they had made their decision about letting them stay or making them go. Several Temple people wanted to find another place. The heart man who had been guiding them said they didn't have enough provisions and were running low on water already. He insisted they had to find some dry land right there.

The Faeries saw the rage light with these people and did not like it, but they also saw other light there that they did like and were unsure what to do about these people. Some of the Faeries wanted to make the mists send them away, but when the Temple people did not go away and did not push their way into the marsh looking for land, but sat meditating instead and began to look toward their inner perceptions to help them find some dry land, many of the Faeries then thought they might be wrong about these people. When the Temple people persisted in their meditation and almost cleared enough mist to show them another patch of dry land, the Faeries saw the Temple people as having some powers similar to their own. The Faeries saw that they were not violent people, and that they had not come to make war. They still felt cautious and uneasy about them for reasons they could not explain, but let them see a little more land to find out what they might try to do there.

The Temple people did not like the unwelcome feeling of their landing, their damp, unsheltered conditions or the dismal surroundings in which they found themselves, but by the time they saw more dry land, they were glad to have anything, felt they had some spiritual power helping them and had begun to like the idea of being that hidden, as though it, also, was meant to be. Something old was being stirred in them about being hidden from My light also. They felt excited for some reason they could not explain, as though there was magic in the air. The Faeries liked that feeling in them, too.

When they found this piece of dry land, the young woman said she was glad, because that was the place she had been guided to and did not think it was right to say anything unless others were guided there also, because the land needed to open to them all, not just her. The others didn't like this. It was her tone more than anything else that bothered them there, and many of them thought she was trying to make a prediction after the fact to look good. She then said that this was all meant to happen, too, because otherwise, the ship would not have brought them to this place.

When they landed, the Temple people did not realize there were any Faeries involved in what had been happening to them, or that there were any local people who might be watching them, but the Faeries told the local people about them, and said that they had given them a cautious reception to see what they were going to do. The local people were very friendly with the Faeries and knew that the Faeries protected them from being found by making them invisible whenever necessary. They were very surprised to hear that the Faeries had allowed the Temple people to be there. In the minds of many of the Temple people, this was a new beginning, and they began it excitedly.

THE NEW TEMPLE

The local people observed these Temple people for a while, too, before they revealed their presence. When they saw the Temple people meditating and fasting, and that they appeared to be running out of the fresh water they had brought with them without making a move to find more, they thought they were not of this world and must be similar to the Faeries. The light in the Temple people was similar to the Faeries except their own light was more golden. The local people made the mistake of thinking that these people were superior to them, and some jealousy arose among them that the Faeries might like these people better and that that was why they let them be there. The local people decided they needed to welcome them and gave them a cautious welcome.

The local people went to them to offer them first water, then food and finally, invited them into their homes when they saw how cold they were from lack of shelter. It was a relief to the Temple people to have help finding the means to sustain themselves, but the local people did not like the way they felt themselves subtly, but almost immediately, treated like servants. The local people, for the most part, did not comment on this and said nothing about the Faeries, but because they felt sure the Faeries had let these people find this place or they could not be there, the Temple people had their respect and acceptance from the beginning more than they knew and for reasons they did not know.

The contrast between the polished stone the Temple people were used to and the "mud huts" with thatched roofs the local people lived in did not lead the Temple people to believe that these people could even be provincial cousins to the powerful Celtic people they had heard about, or that they could be a people who already knew a lot of the things they knew or even a people who had any power or magic at all. The local people were not ready to let them know any of these things, either. They presented as they had always presented; humble people living at the edge of a marshland and nothing more.

When the Temple people said they wanted to live there and offered the local people gold to build them a Temple, the local people found this laughable. They told the Temple people that they had no use for gold other than to make ornaments from it. When they heard the plans of what the Temple people wanted to have built, they told the Temple people that there was no rock nearby that they had plans to haul or were going to haul and that they certainly weren't going to spend time polishing stone. They felt more than reluctant.

The local people, and the Faeries, had begun to feel deep stirrings of old memories that seemed to be of another Temple that had been there in ancient, Atlantean times, and they hadn't liked its presence. They had only ancient stories they told that had been handed down from so long ago, that while they didn't want another "Temple," they also did not want to judge these people because of old memories. Nonetheless, there was something similar enough that it was eliciting a reaction in them. They told the Temple people a Temple already existed and that they would take them to see Stonehenge at the Spring Equinox. When the Temple people asked them if people lived there, the locals said that they didn't need to live at a Temple because the Earth was their Temple.

That Spring, the Equinox celebration they had planned was not as grand as they had hoped. The weather was rather cold and dismal compared to what they were used to in Greece, and they did not have their own place to live, but that was when the local people showed them how they marked the dates at Stonehenge and where the Sun rose that day. The Temple people thought it was crude compared to the way they marked the dates at home, but it seemed to be accurate enough. They were invited to participate in the local festivities, and, although it was not the kind of sex their fantasies had envisioned, some of them snuck away after dark to have sex. They noticed there seemed to be other people who were off by themselves. They did not realize that the local people allowed young people thinking of getting married to have sex on these same days to see if they felt they were right for one another. The Temple people took this to mean that the local people were much looser with their sexual relationships than they actually were.

After the Spring Equinox, the Temple people were in agreement, for the most part, that Stonehenge was crudely formed compared to Temples at home. They gave up on their plans for a large Temple and decided to settle for anything the local people were willing to build, which was one large, round wattle and daub room with dwellings nearby. They wanted to move along rapidly with their plans, and they wanted to be ready to have the celebration they had envisioned when the time for observance of the Summer Solstice came. They had been living near a hill and had seen another one nearby that they thought would be perfect for what they had in mind. It was the Tor of Glastonbury, but they did not know that. When they said they wanted to go there, the local Celtic people, at first, said that it wasn't used for anything because it was too hard to get to. "All the more perfect," the Temple people thought and made plans to find a way to get there.

When they could not find the way through the marshes, they went to the local people and told them they wanted them to take them there because they had made plans to terrace the hillside and try to grow grapes. The more the Temple people insisted they wanted to do this, the more the local people did not know what to say.

The Faeries had already come to the local people and said they did not want these people on the Tor. The local people did not want to mention the Faeries because the Temple people had not mentioned them, which meant to them that the Faeries had not allowed themselves to be seen by these newcomers. The local people went to the Faeries and told all of this to them. The Faeries told them to tell the Temple people that there wasn't enough sun or heat to grow their grapes and that they would have to drink Meade like everyone else. The Temple people told them they wanted to try anyway. The Celtic people told the Temple people they used the Tor for their own sacred processions and rituals and that it must be left as a sacred place.

It bothered the Temple people when they could not get the local people to do what they wanted. They were anxious to go ahead with their plans. The local Celtic people did not want to feel pressured to give them the Tor. The local people were feeling somewhat rolled over by these Temple people, but the pleasantness with which they presented their plans was confusing the guilt they did have there into feeling that their feelings were wrong. They didn't want to judge the Temple people because that didn't feel loving to them. They showed them another location, but the Temple people wanted the hill because it was drier land and they thought they could grow grapes there. They told the Temple people their next celebration was Beltane and invited the Temple people to join them in that.

Some of the Temple people liked the idea of another celebration halfway between the Spring Equinox and the Summer Solstice, but many of them didn't want to be distracted from their purpose and wanted to find a way to go ahead with plans to build their own Temple. They said they still wanted to grow grapes and needed to get their seeds in the ground. The local people and the Faeries both liked this light that wanted to grow things and have sacred places, honor nature and other of the many things the Temple people were saying. The Temple people were careful to be pleasant instead of pushy about their plans, and tried to get the local people interested and even enthusiastic about them, thinking they would like to have their horizons widened. The local people, at the insistence of the Faerie King, did not give way to the Temple people, and in the end, agreed to the let them plant their grapes on a nearby hill and build their Temple at the foot of that hill. They did make it round and the local people did help them, but the Faeries wished they had not insisted on making their presence obvious. They had a bad feeling about it.

The Temple people wanted to have their own rituals and processions. They also wanted to have the kind of sex they wanted to have, but they did not want this to be seen or known by the local people, not only because they had presented as not having sex, but also because of some of the things that some of the men wanted to do to some of the women. Many had wanted to come dressed in the images of the Greek gods and goddesses, but given the local nature-based approach to rituals and the feelings of Pan that were stirred there, it did not take them long to get the idea that they could dress up like trees, flowers, plants and animals. They wanted to make the focus of the Summer Solstice the power of the Sun to draw nature into its full force, or presence, as they preferred to call it. To them, Apollo was very masculine, and therefore phallic. Some of the men saw this as their opportunity to do anything they could think of to draw the women out and into a full orgasm. Dressing up like animals was a good way for the men to behave like animals, themselves, and if the women wanted to be plants, well, then they could eat them. Flowers were especially sexually enticing to them.

The festival was going to be dedicated to the Sun and also to the Greek god of fertility, wine and drama, Dionysus. Many wanted to dress in his image, but the Heart man, who had become the Head of the Temple after all, said he should be the only one to dress that way. The rest of the men, then, decided to be Satyrs or Centaurs, but some decided to be predatory animals. The local people were planning to have a procession all the way to Stonehenge, followed by merrymaking and eating as usual, and when the local people departed, the Temple people, who had not seen the Faeries yet, thought they were alone there. They were glad, because now they could have the celebration they really wanted to have. They wanted to make the most of it, but they did not want to outrage the local people, either.

The Temple people started early, as soon as they decided they could feel the forces of nature rising to greet the Sun. Their procession slowly spiraled through their vineyard and up the hill, calling upon the favors of the various deities they wanted to invoke there. They were at the top of the hill when the Sun rose. Although they could no longer do form change, they had created costumes. They had no wine yet, but Meade would do this first year, and they had learned a little about local plants, and especially the mushrooms, and decided to include some in their Meade to "enhance its properties," as they said then.

As afternoon came on, they began to have the sex they really wanted to have, role playing as though they actually were what they were dressed to be, doing whatever they wanted to do and making whatever noises they wanted to make, as though they were animals. There were more flowers among them than it appeared from their discussions there were going to be, and the ones dressed as animals preyed upon them. They considered it fun to take these Temple members down, as though they were stalking or hunting them, and then have sex with them. Some of them growled and slobbered and drooled and actually bit their partners in some places. The Moon was full, and the men who had fastened onto the word "anything" on the ship now felt it was finally their chance to do anything they wanted to do sexually, and they had their potions of Meade and psychedelic mushrooms to loosen up any inhibitions they had. Most of the "flowers" screamed, loudly at times, many of the things that had been said in the Purple gap, and none of them admitted to liking any of it. Many of the men were unsure what to do then, but a number of them silenced it by forcing themselves down their partner's throat.

The Faeries saw this and did not like it. They did not like the light that arose from this, and saw that this light was being turned loose on the land. To the Temple people, this first celebration of their own had been grand, and most of them were happy. The weather was warm, the Sun was shining, the rains were falling gently down, the mists were hiding them at night and all appeared to be well with life and the good Earth. The local people came home from their pilgrimage to Stonehenge, and when they saw the happiness of the Temple people, they thought that this day had been a good experience for them all.

Then, the Faeries came to the local people and told them they had seen a light they did not like arising from the hill where the Temple people were and had gone to see what was causing it. Although they did not tell the local, Celtic people what was causing it, they told the local people that they did not like what they saw. To them, this light was more of the kind they had felt cautious about when they first saw the Temple people. The Faeries feared this light and told the local people they feared what it was going to do and where it might settle in. The local people began to realize, then, how many things they hadn't liked about the Temple people and had overlooked it because the Faeries had let them be there.

The Faeries were very upset that they had let these Temple people in, and the local people were upset that they had helped them. They wanted the Temple people to leave, but now the problem was that the Temple people had gotten themselves established there. The Faeries and the local people didn't quite feel that their feelings of uneasiness were enough to make them leave, and how could they do that anyway?

The Faeries didn't want to say what they saw, and especially now that their distrust of the Temple people had returned, they did not want to reveal themselves to the Temple people. Their guilt did not allow them to stand firm that their feelings were enough. After all, they had let these Temple people in, and even liked them in many ways.

They decided to watch it a little more, and the local people decided they must find out what these Temple people were really doing there.

When the Temple people first began to give classes, the local people had little interest in the Greek knowledge the Temple people were imparting, but some of them attended their classes with the intention of learning more about these people. The Temple people were not expecting the local people to already know so much about what they were "teaching" them. The local people viewed these "classes" more as an exchange than as actual classes. The Temple people did not see it this way so much as they viewed themselves as teachers. The local people did not like the tone of superiority from the Temple people. When the local people approached the Temple people about this, the Temple people were more than polite and accommodating. The Celtic people did not trust this. When the Celtic people told them as much, the Temple people told the local people that it had not been their intent to offend, but said it in a way that implied the local people were being unfair. They assured them that they had heard their complaints, would look into them and would make any shifts that were necessary to keep the good relationship they had been having there, but it was only form changes they gave them, not a real shift.

The Celts were much more direct emotionally, as a people, and had not found the necessity to surface many of their feelings in words because they understood one another quite well at the feeling level, but they were confused by these subtle feelings of superiority and guilt they were feeling from the Temple people. The Temple people withheld many things from the local people. Overall, they were viewing themselves as a more developed people, almost as though they were missionaries ministering to a "primitive" population. They viewed the local people as unable to comprehend what they were really doing in their rituals and ceremonies, and gave them no real information about any of this.

The Temple people wanted to gain the local people's trust, and thought the way to do this was through a presentation of mutual respect by showing interest in the local nature-based approach, but the local people didn't want to give this information to the Temple people. When tempers flared, the Temple people usually withdrew into meditation and did not notice how the way in which they did this left the local people with a feeling that they were being viewed as spiritually inferior or wrong somehow in what had taken place there. The presentation the Temple people were making was not building the trust they wanted, and they did not know why.

Meanwhile, as word was spreading about the existence of this Temple, people began to come from other places to see what was happening there. The Temple people's pride in what they were doing was going to be their downfall, because the Temple people didn't know that talk about them was reaching all the way to Rome. The uneasiness in the local people tried to get the Temple people to move to a more central location so people could come there more easily, but the Temple people didn't want to leave their vineyard.

Many times, the young woman, who was now their High Priestess, enraged them with her rage-laden comments. They would often go away asking one another if they had heard it in the same way after she would make comments to them. When the Temple people did not listen to them with what they considered to be mutual respect and understanding, the local people held back their rage that wanted to get rid of them and presented silence to the Temple people; a silence they thought would unnerve them, but the Temple people took it as acquiescence or compliance.

Herbs were an important study, and some of the Temple people were very interested in the herbal knowledge of the local people. Their studies began as an exploration of local plants for food and medicine but soon got sidetracked by old stirrings that Pangea was a place of partying and lots of sex; wild and free sex with unnamed partners out in the woods at night, and if not unnamed, then masked would do. Soon, they were not as interested in herbs as medicine for healing as much as they were in what became a quest for brews to prevent or end pregnancies or to produce more and more powerful orgasms, along with psychedelics and other sensory distortions.

While, at first, the Temple people felt sure they could make unwanted pregnancies abort by meditating, as time went on, they were having more and more problems with pregnancies because they were having more and more sex with less and less spiritual focus and consciousness involved. In the name of herbal studies, some Temple people began asking local people about herbs for birth control or abortion, but they did not seem to know of any that were really effective and had their own methods that did not seem to be effective for the Temple people. It was an awkward subject since the Temple people were not admitting they had sex or pregnancies, even though the local people suspected as much.

Since they were not admitting they were having these pregnancies, they were handling this by having the women go into "meditative seclusion," as they referred to it. They thought they had been abandoning the results of their unwanted pregnancies, as had often been done in Greece at that time, in such deep and hidden places in the marshes that they did not think they would be found, but the local people moved around in those marshes more than the Temple people knew. The local people did not suspect the kind of sex the Temple people were having, but they knew they were lying about having sex because they had begun to find little "lost" babies in the marshlands. In their hearts, they could not leave them out there, exposed to the elements to die. The Temple people denied knowing anything about these babies. When the Temple people would not claim any knowledge of these babies, the local people began to raise them themselves and decided not to let the Temple people know about it.

The Temple people continued to tell themselves they had no problems in the world that couldn't be solved by correct spiritual practices. They did not think they had any emotional problems with the local people. When the local people showed declining interest in Temple classes and functions, the Temple people, for the most part, viewed them as "reverting" to their old ways and not ready to understand what the Temple people had to offer them there. The Temple people went to the village less often, and the local people went to the Temple less often. Meanwhile, the Temple babies were growing up in nearby villages.

Some of the Temple people could sense that something was amiss with the local people, but delayed going to the villages. When they did go, they saw some children who looked strangely Greek to them. At first they thought local women had been having sex with some of the Temple men, but as time went on, they began to realize that this was not the case. The Temple people did not stop having the kind of sex they wanted to have on their special days, but they began to kill these babies instead of putting them out in the marshes.

The Temple people wanted to have fun at night and still do their normal Temple functions and spiritual practices during the day, but more and more, their nature interests were in how to tap into the power of the land and its plants and animals to have super orgasms. They were blowing themselves away like the explosion in Blue without realizing what was happening to them. They began to party and play music more and more in the woods at night.

The local people didn't like it. Even though they sometimes wanted to join them, they thought the Temple people were partying too much and making too much noise. Some of the children thought their parents were being the equivalent of old-fashioned and rigid. The local people, at least, wanted it to end earlier than the Temple people ended it. Then, when it grew to be daybreak, the Temple people were not around to help with any of the work it took to sustain them all. They had begun to think that gold was all they needed to contribute, and some of this gold, also, was finding its way to Rome.

The Temple people claimed they were busy at night with their rituals of the Moon, which had many phases and to which their Temple was now, also, dedicated. They told themselves this was alright because it was all ritual of some sort or another and all dedicated to something. The more things went on with the Temple people, though, the more disquieted the Faeries became. They told the local people they did not like the noise or Temple people all about in the woods at night. It disrupted their dances, did not let nature rest the way it needed to rest, and in the end, was not respectful to nature, no matter how much they said all of this was dedicated to nature. They also told the local people that the populations of certain plants were being decimated and only the ones they knew to have certain properties, so they knew what the Temple people were doing. The Faeries were adamant that they did not like the light being generated there by the Temple people.

The Faeries had also found that there was now light of this sort under the Tor, which meant to them that Temple people had found and were going into their sacred caves under the Tor. It seemed to the Faeries that all of them were in danger of being taken over by this light. The local people aligned with the Faeries on this. They did not like all of the noise and hoopla going on in the woods at night and were growing weary of losing sleep. They particularly did not like having their children hear this.

The Temple people were polite and friendly in their response to the complaints of the locals, telling them they understood their problem and would do their best to keep the noise away from their villages. The Temple people sounded reasonable and helpful, but the local people didn't like the way it felt, which is what they went by more than what was said. Nothing really changed with the behavior of the Temple people. The men in the Temple often didn't even remember what they had done, but they were not willing to give this up. They decided to go farther from the local villages, but then they found that they were near other villages. They decided they needed to restrain themselves except when the local people went on their pilgrimages to Stonehenge.

Then came the Autumnal Equinox, and the local people announced that they planned to stay home and wanted to participate in the Temple people's rituals and festivities. They knew others from the area were planning to come also. They were all expecting a good harvest of grapes and thought surely they were going to find out what good wine tasted like. The Temple people hadn't realized this could be a natural outcome of their extending reputation. They were not happy about this, but they did not want to show the local people anything other than happiness about it. They told them that good wine had to age a long time and that there was no wine ready yet that they considered to be good wine. The local people didn't know about this, but they had to accept that the Temple people were not going to offer any of their wine to anyone except, maybe, to themselves.

Still, there were going to be people there. The Temple people told the local people that they would be welcome. Privately, they felt that now they were going to have to make plans to have their sex somewhere away from the local people. The problem was that there was nowhere to go other than marshland. Boats didn't seem like any fun for what they had in mind. This was when the new High Priestess told them she had found caves under the Tor, and that she thought they could go there. When she told them she had been in these caves and that the caves glowed, the others thought these caves could be perfect. There was going to be no Moon that night. The local people, they thought, would go home early because of no Moon. She thought she could lead them there even if there were mists, and they would be more hidden than usual.

When the day came, the Temple gave everyone a small taste of their wine, like a wine tasting. They told them all that it would taste much better when it was properly aged, which would not even be the next year. They told them that if they went to their own festivities, the next year after that their wine might be ready. Meanwhile, the Temple people had their own potions in their cups, which they did not mention and did not share. When the dusk of evening began to settle around them, the local people made some bonfires and began to sing and dance around them. The Temple people realized they were in for a long wait. Most of them decided to join in the singing and dancing, and as altered as their consciousness was by their potions, many of them began to lose track of where they really were.

The local women were adorned with flowers and leaves, and all the people were in a happy mood. The Temple people were much more elaborately costumed as mythological creatures, flowers and even some trees. Some of the Temple people's costumes had been designed to leave their sexual parts exposed, as in nature. They had covered this up for the day, but now, some of them began taking these coverings off. The local people were not pleased at such a public display.

The Head of the Temple saw that he needed to talk to his people and remind them of where they were. When some of them did not want to comply, the Head of the Temple apologized to the local people, saying that some of his people were quite drunk, and that he needed to take them back to the Temple along with the others in case anyone else was more drunk than he thought. Gathering the Temple people, he noticed they were not all there. He told the ones he had found to go to the Temple, and he would soon follow. He tried to find the others, but could not and felt very distressed that this was going to make a problem for the Temple.

The local people were rather dismayed and disappointed. "Perhaps it is because the Moon is not full," they said to themselves, but later that night, after they went home, they began to have terrible feelings and strange dreams they did not want to share with one another, but felt they had to.

In the morning, the Faerie King came to them. He was most furious that the Temple people had gone into the caves under the Tor, and had done things he would not talk about. He would only say that they needed to run the

Temple people out of their land. The Faerie King said they had to go back to wherever they came from. Then, one of the Temple children who had been growing up with the local people as parents said that if there was a problem, he thought they should solve it themselves and not put it off on other people. He did not know he was a Temple child, but he spoke right to the guilt the local people had there.

The local people talked among themselves about what to do. Many times they had tried to talk to the Temple people about their concerns, but had not had much success. Many times, they had talked among themselves about trying to move the Temple people out of their area. It was usually the Temple children who talked in favor of letting the Temple people stay; children the local people had raised as their own children. These children had such a way of pointing out the good things the Temple people were doing, and did not seem to take the feelings of their parents very seriously. When these children had wanted to go and study at the Temple, their parents had tried to deter them.

The Temple children often responded with things like, "We like it that people come here from other places to study with the Temple people. We want to meet them and to know what they are teaching at the Temple. You think the Faeries are so wise you let them tell you what to do all the time. The Faeries let them come here, so it must have been meant to happen."

Their parents did not know what to say, other than that they had feelings about such things, sometimes long in advance of them ever really happening. These children scorned such things and said that if they sat around expecting the worst, sooner or later, something they didn't like would happen, and then their parents would say, "See, we told you so."

The local people decided to go to the Temple people with their complaints once again. Once again, the Temple people were very accommodating, but this time, the local people demanded more than polite response. They had had too much of that only to have nothing really change. They told them they knew they had gone into the caves under the Tor and that they knew those were absolutely forbidden to them.

One young mother told them that they had found babies in the marshes that they were sure were the result of pregnancies the Temple people claimed to never have, and that they had been raising them as their own children. She also told them that some of them now wanted to come to the Temple to study and that they were not going to allow it unless there was a real change in the Temple. The local people made it clear that they wanted a change in the Temple or else they wanted the Temple people to leave.

The ones they were speaking to told them it was mostly the High Priestess who was the problem and that it had been her idea to go into the caves under the Tor. They said they didn't want any feelings of hostility she had stirred among the local people to reflect on them. They told the High Priestess that displeasing the local people could not be tolerated anymore, because it was the local people upon whose hospitality their continued presence depended. They used the situation with the local people to displace the one who had appointed herself High Priestess on the ship and appointed another High Priestess. They presented this as a position shift, but it was not a real position shift. They just became more secretive about what they were really doing.

The local people reluctantly let their Temple children go to the Temple to study. The Temple people did not acknowledge them as their own children, even though they knew that they must be. These children were Celtic in many ways. The Temple people saw them as children who had desire to learn what they knew and the mental acuity to do it that many of the local people didn't seem to have. They acknowledged and rewarded them as students from the Celtic people who could learn what they had to teach and thought that they finally had some students who were going to tell them more of what they really wanted to know about the local Celtic and Druid people.

The Temple people began to see these students of theirs as the ones who could perpetuate the Temple. When they managed to initiate them into the Temple even though their parents objected, they told the young people that part of their mission was to go back to the local people to learn as much as they could there, because one of the missions of the Temple was the bringing together of both worlds. This made it seem to these children that their parents were resisting this grand and altruistic mission and purpose and that these children had a destiny to be the bridges between the two worlds.

In perpetuating the Temple, the Temple people gave the most prominent positions in the Temple to the children who were most like them and who they thought were most likely to perpetuate the Temple the way they wanted it perpetuated. The Temple people showed these children only the classes they taught and certain spiritual practices such as meditation and never let them see the sorts of rituals in which they had been conceived until they were older and tested by many other rituals and initiations to make sure they were going to be like them in these ways, too.

Since no babies had been found for quite a while, some of the local people hoped they had gotten their point across in a way that had caused a behavior change, but others feared that what the Faerie King had said about the Temple people meant that they were doing something more than just going into the caves under the Tor, something really terrible, but they did not know how to find out. Their children did not tell them anything too terrible, and when the Temple people presented themselves as such calm and friendly people most of the time and when so many of their "own children" were becoming Temple people now, they did not think they could accuse them of anything. The Faerie King was beside himself about it, saying the local people were not wrong in their feelings. Something terrible was going on there.

Then, one night, the Faerie King came to a local man and asked him to go with him into the marshes. The Faerie King led the man to a place and asked him to wait there until he came back. The man waited a long time. All he knew was that the Faerie King was flying around the area looking for something.

The Faerie King knew that the local people's complaints had caused the Temple people to do things farther away. Out on the moors, the Faerie King found the Temple woman he was looking for. She had just given birth, but no baby. He flew around nearby, but there was nothing there. He flew further and found a man who was just putting the baby down on the moor, rather gently, as though he was reluctant to leave it. The man walked back toward the woman, and the Faerie King flew back to get the Celtic man, urging him to follow as quickly as he could. The Faerie King was flying out ahead and circling back, protecting the baby this way so that nothing would happen to him before the man could get there. The man did not like having to go so far out onto the moors by himself that late at night, but he felt guided and protected by the Faerie King.

The Faerie King led the man to the baby and urged him to take the baby home to his wife. The man did not like the idea. They already had troubles from the Temple children, and he already had many children, but neither could he bring himself to leave the child there. When he brought the child home, his wife, at first, said, "Oh, No!" But, she gazed into the child's eyes, and soon said, "Oh, what's one more?"

This baby was only twelve years old when He begged his parents to let Him go and study with the Temple people, but He considered himself to be a man. His parents refused to allow this for as long as they could, telling Him they were not good people there, but He appeared not to believe them and seemed even more intent on going. When his parents saw that they could not deter Him, his father began to physically train Him to protect Himself. He learned what they had to teach Him, and then, one morning, they found that He had taken His things and was gone.

The boy did not know why He must go to the Temple, but He could not hold Himself back anymore. He walked several hours to get to the Temple, was very young and had come alone, but He was eager to learn, so they let Him stay. At first they didn't know He was a Temple child because they hadn't been letting that happen anymore, but his real mother was curious about Him because of where He came from and felt drawn to become one of His teachers.

When He began to read, He felt like a sponge for the information they gave Him there. He soon became one of their more treasured students because of His aptitude and eagerness to learn and soak up their ways, but as He read, He also began to feel that some of the things recorded in their books were not right, and He began to ask questions and point these things out to them. Some did not like His questions, but when He became a little older, others allowed him to read their older and rarer books that had been brought from Delphi. He began to have feelings, not only that He knew what was in these books, but that He had actually written them. He had already learned about reincarnation, and He began to consider that He might be the reincarnated author of these books. He began to do His own writings.

His actual father was not there anymore, but his mother was, and she began to think that this must be her son. He was the right age but He had never been told about the circumstances of His own birth. She did not tell Him, either, but she began to take more interest in Him and became His ally in the Temple. When He told her of His feelings about their books, she did not think He was wrong. He asked her to tell Him everything she could about the trip they had made to come there, but she could not tell Him much. All she was able to tell Him was what she had been told by his father, which was not much. She told Him that, for some reason, they were not supposed to talk about this and were forbidden to write it down. She said that the Temple people preferred to say they were from the stars.

Meanwhile, the local people were becoming more and more worried that the "bad light" there, as they called it now, was drawing something to them that they did not want. They were already hearing tales of the Romans and their spreading dominance. They began to hear of the Romans advancing in their direction. Then, they began to hear woeful tales of what this meant for the local people.

The Temple people did not respond with worry. They had, long ago, decided that these tales of Roman cruelty were born of the earlier High Priestess's prejudice toward Romans. They thought that even if Romans did manage to come into the surrounding area, the mists would protect them. The local people feared this might not be true for long, especially if the Faerie King withdrew his protection, as he had been threatening to do. The Faerie King had even talked of moving his people somewhere else.

By then, the Temple children knew about the Faeries because so many of them had been raised with them and had played with them along with the other local children. They considered the Faeries to be their friends and allies, but took this more for granted than the Faeries felt to be true. The Temple children did not know how precarious the Faeries' protection had become, and their parents did not want to let them know this. The Faerie King had threatened withdrawal of his protection so many times around issues involving the Temple that most of the Temple children thought it was only another way he controlled their parents.

If they had the protection of the Faeries, as they believed they did, they thought it was unconditional. To them, unconditional love was being accepted unconditionally no matter what they did and accepting whatever others did unconditionally. If they did not like something, they moved away from it. This was what this child did when His adopted family told Him they didn't want Him to study at the Temple. It was, to them, not a matter of how people felt or He would have wondered more about how His parents felt when He left them. They did not understand how feelings fit in that were not within their own definition of love and judged against them according to their imprinting, even though they had been raised differently. To the local people, having love reciprocated meant not wanting to do things that did not feel good to the others involved, but to these children, that was guilt.

The local Druid people were quite angry. They felt that the Temple people had something to do with why the

Romans were advancing in their direction. Distrust was increasing in them and in other local people. The Druids did not have as much guilt as the Celts did there, and openly disliked the Temple people, who they felt, were trying to displace them as the most learned people in the area and dismiss their spiritual knowledge and guidance.

The Summer Solstice was coming. In that year, the two days of the Full Moon fell on the day before the Summer Solstice and on the Solstice. The Temple people were making plans to have this be their biggest celebration ever, starting a full day ahead with their Moon rituals and moving toward the Sun on the Solstice with a full procession through their vineyards and up their hill. Things had gone even further out than they had in the beginning. By the time the deep indigo evening of the longest day of the year had settled in around them and the Full Moon rose, first golden and then white, they had been partying, drinking their concoctions and having sex for twenty-four hours. Some of the men were so drunk and drugged that they did not know what was happening around them or what they were really doing.

Some of the local people still went to this festival, hoping their children would not go so far out into a drugged orgy if they were present, but many others had continued to go to Stonehenge because they had given up. Nearby, the Faeries were dancing in the moonlight. They could hear the sounds from the Temple people and, once again, did not like hearing this or seeing the light that was rising from them. There were some Temple children at the festival who saw the Faeries' light and tried to call the Faeries to come join them. The Faerie King and some of the other Faeries rose in the air to look over and see what was really going on there.

Most of the Faeries were quite terrified. Feeling he must startle them out of their shock, the Faerie King yelled at the other Faeries to fly away with him. When they reached another hill, they still wanted to dance, believing that if they did not dance, nature would not be vitalized the way it needed to be, but they could not. The evening's mood had been suddenly changed for them. They had fears that part of this light had attached itself to them in some way, and when they looked around, it seemed to be true. A panic arose in them, and especially in the ones who had more of this light, that they were now going to descend into being mortals and no longer live forever. They believed that to remain as they were, they had to keep themselves entirely separate from what they saw as causing the descent into physical density and mortality.

The Faeries began to feel that they must dance now and try to dance it out of themselves for their own sakes, but they did not want it to go out into nature this way. They did not know what to do with it. The Faeries began to dance in a tight circle, trying to purify the light so they could send it out into nature again. So focused were they that they did not notice that some of the Satyr-like men were sneaking up on them. Suddenly, their dancing was abruptly and rudely interrupted by these men leaping out of the woods and trying to grab them. They reacted quickly, rising high in the air. They were not solid enough for these men to hold onto them, but some of the Faeries were touched by the "bad light" these men had.

The Faeries did not know which way to fly. The Faerie King felt furious at the situation and feared he now had some of this rage in himself. The Faeries were as if frozen in the air, and he feared he was seeing them all sinking down into the grasp of these Satyr men. He exhorted them, "Fly!" and suddenly Faeries were flying every which way in a panic.

The Faerie King was furious with himself that he had not listened to his original feelings about these Temple people. "You had to find out! You just had to know!" he kept saying to himself as he went after his Faeries, telling himself that he did not have to know; he just had to feel that something was wrong and act on it, but even then he wasn't sure if this would have been heartless toward these people. Old memories were being stirred in him, too; images of running and flying away, almost stampeded over by others who were also running and flying away. Where they had run to was this place, but where they had run from, he did not remember. He had memories of Faeries and Elves running free, but he could not remember what happened to them. It must have been this kind of thing, he thought, but why? He thought of the caves and wanted to go there with the Faeries. Then, he realized these people were probably in there, too. He did not mind mortals, but mortals with no respect, he did greatly mind.

They ran deeper into the woods then, moving more in terror as they went than moving terror, but they could not get away from this light. It went with them wherever they went, and wherever it settled in, it seemed able to increase its presence. The Faeries didn't know how it was able to do this. They were terrified that it was not possible to ever go back to the way they were before this happened to them. The Faerie King feared he and his people were contaminated now, and he did not know the cure. He felt the Temple people must be stopped somehow or made to leave and take their "bad" light with them, but he didn't know who would help him now that his Faeries were contaminated. The Faeries were quarreling and blaming and showing other signs of lack of alignment. They didn't dance anymore that night, and the Faerie King saw it as a bad omen.

Late the next day the Faerie King went to the village. When he told them what had happened and that they didn't dance much that night, the villagers feared for their crops and for everything else they depended on from their land. The Faerie King said a lot more things to the villagers, and some of it I am repeating here. "I have failed. I can no longer protect you. I can't even protect myself and the other Faeries. I don't know what to do. You've been becoming more like your Temple children's light, and now I, and the rest of the Faeries, have also been contaminated with it.

When we first took them in, we had our doubts. I wish we had acted then. When we took their unwanted babies in as "lost" babies, we thought we were saving them from something, and we were! Horrible things! But, only temporarily. We thought they would grow up to be more like us, but, they have been becoming more and more like the Temple people, and now they are making us more like them, until now, we are all contaminated by their presence. All those Temple people think they know better than all of us! They are not loving people. They have no respect for others. I see no way to bridge the gap between us. We have to make them leave, somehow. I don't know how because we've become entangled with them. I don't want to protect the Temple people, and I'm not sure I can make any of us invisible anymore. I'm sorry I didn't have the heart to let them starve out there in the marshes or frighten them into going somewhere else."

The Faerie King said many more words, and was deeply, deeply troubled, as were most of the villagers. There were some Temple children there, however, and most of them had feelings that the Faerie King's protection hadn't really been anything more than behavior control.

The Faerie King began to jump around and repeat things to himself. "I don't know why I didn't remember this! I don't know why I didn't remember this!" as though he was remembering it just then. "It has been so long! You mortals don't remember this and have even quit telling these stories, but I should not have forgotten! They have never listened to us; they have only pretended to!" He was getting more and more agitated, flying up and down, back and forth, almost as though he was going to run away in that moment.

"I fear I have failed all of our people now! There's no hope other than to stay completely separate from them! I should never have let them in! How could I have let myself forget? It was too much for me! I couldn't stand to look at it! I couldn't stand to look at it! I should have realized it in time to get safely away again. I don't know where to go! Everywhere I look, we've all been touched! We must never let ourselves be touched! Where to go, where to go? Stampedes! Animals and everyone running in fear! A wizard, a mean wizard! We do not like him! He's not high, he's low! A mean man! We must stay completely away! Run north, run north! No, run south, run south! Hide in the green places! No! He hates the green places! He fireballs the green places! He sends his mean ones to destroy us! I must take my Faeries and run! We must fly quickly away! I don't know where to go! Everything is burning around us! There's nowhere to go, but we must go! They lie! They teach bad things! We didn't act when I found out about them. Now look what's happening to us all! We're about to be invaded by Romans!"

The local people were terribly frightened. They were clumped together, trying to remember what the Faerie King was talking about and figure out what to do. They could not remember, and a great silence had fallen on them. The local people did not want to believe this about children they had raised, but they could not disbelieve it, either. The group was quiet for some time, considering this. Then they said, "You let them in here originally, and then we were involved with them, and none of us could ever quite make ourselves run them out, leave their babies to die or kill them. What are we going to do! Please don't leave us! Help us!"

Soon after that, the Temple man, who was the reincarnation of the head of the Temple at Delphi, now a grown man, came home from the Temple for a visit. The villagers were glum and worried. At first they didn't know if they trusted Him anymore, but when they told Him what had been happening there, He also seemed to be very upset. He did not want to believe it and told himself that this could not be true. He did not believe the Temple people were unloving and did not want to believe that the sex they were having there was rage sex or unloving. He had wanted to believe that it was free abandon, and did not want to believe the Faerie King was right, or that the Faerie King knew more than He did. When they all persisted with Him that things had gone too far and that something bad was being drawn to them, He consulted the Druids who agreed with the other local people. Finally, He told them He must go back for the people who would come with Him and for the old books.

They all opposed Him saying, no, only He could stay, and that if any others were going to come, they had to come of their own accord. When the reincarnated Head of the Temple at Delphi told them more about the books and assured them these were history books and records He had made long ago, and was making now. He said that He would keep them well-hidden and only show them to those they really trusted. At first they said, "No, only oral tradition," but then they were all reminded of the problem their own memory loss had just reflected to them. When He said the Druids were interested in the books and that He did not want to lose them again, they decided to let Him bring the books, even thinking they might also let Him write down some things about them.

When this young man got back to the Temple, He did not think He liked the idea of a split in the Temple people. He had had resistance when He was listening to what the Faerie King and the Celtic and Druid people had to say there, but did give Himself the freedom to bring back with Him whoever He chose to bring. When the Faerie King was furious with Him over this, He did not like it and said that whoever wanted to come must be allowed to come. The Faerie King disliked being put in this position so much that he and the rest of the Faeries were just suddenly not there anymore and no one knew where they went. Now, this young man was very angry at the Faerie King.

All across Gaul, certain Roman officers had heard tantalizing stories about a Temple people in the West from somewhere far away, "maybe even the stars," some said, who had some kind of a university, hidden in the mists and unfindable except by those who were meant to go there. There, there was supposed to be lots of gold and a bridge between two worlds, one of which, they thought must be the underworld, since they had heard stories about things going on underground there, too. They began to think that at least something of these stories must be true, and they wanted to find this place. They had invaded all of Britain never finding it, even though they had been told where it was supposed to be. They beat their way back and forth through the marshes several times, cutting pathways as they went, intent on finding this place, but even so, they never could. Back they came again and again, and one day, the mists seemed to evaporate in the sunlight and they saw a nearby hill with a vineyard on it. They had heard that the Temple made wine, and they decided to go over there and see what they could find.

They found the Temple, although, at first, they didn't think so. It didn't look like any Temples they had seen before, but the people seemed strangely unlike the local people, and so, they decided this must be the place. They didn't do anything at first, but act interested and curious. They looked around for a while, and then, left some men there to start fires to guide them back if they became lost in the mists. This did not work. The men soon decided that the mists were too dense for fires to be helpful and began to drink the wines and potions the Temple people were giving them.

The others had gone to look around the area. They found the village, but the people weren't there. They found their way back to the Temple and questioned some of the Temple people, finding out where some of the villagers might be. They also began to drink wine laced with potions with some of the Temple people, and pretty soon, began to tell them the stories they'd heard about them. Then, they wanted to know where the gold was. The reincarnated Head of the Temple at Delphi had taken most of the gold with the feeling that He should hide it. The Temple people denied having any gold. The Romans still wanted to know where, then, the gold was. "Traded away," the Temple people said unanimously. The Romans didn't believe them.

These Romans began to search the area and found some of the local people. They were furious as though everyone there had been playing games with them hiding in the mists, and accused them of using magic. The people didn't know why finding them was so important to the Romans and did not know they had heard stories of the Temple and of gold. Gold was not important to the local people, and they didn't understand why gold would be so important to these men.

Without the Faerie King to protect them, they feared the Roman's rage and did not know what to do. When the villagers looked so stupid about gold, this infuriated these Romans even more. They began to be aggressive in their questioning, and when that didn't get them anywhere, they began to intensify their techniques of interrogation. They rounded up the local people they had found, gave them no food or water and did not allow them to talk to one another. They interrogated them one by one, telling each of them that other nearby people had betrayed their location, and then that family and friends they had already interrogated had told them many things so there was no reason to protect anyone by thinking it was helpful to withhold information. They decided to apply some torture to "encourage cooperation, and began to do things that these people had never imagined possible for people to do to other people.

These Roman men got more information than they thought they were going to get, and even heard about the Faerie King and how he used to protect these people. Sensing splits in the people, they began to play them against one another, and as they drank more wine laced with potions, their torturing intensified until it was more for the sport of it than for any further information they could get. When they had already raped the women and some of the men, forcing the children to watch it, they began to torture children and force parents to torture their own children, or any children.

They weren't finding out about any vast amount of gold, and this was bothering them. They found out about the caves under the Tor and took the people in there; sure this was where they were going to find gold. When they didn't, they didn't believe the people that there was no gold in those caves and tortured them even more. They were also torturing Temple people, and relented on any who said they were not opposed to Roman presence and would cooperate with them any way they could. When they felt they could get nothing more, or the people were dead, they piled them up, stacked wood around them, ignited it with dung and burned the bodies.

The young man had gone with some of the villagers to hide His books and what was left of the Temple treasure. When He got feelings not to return to the village, He did not return, but others who were with Him did. They were soon grabbed by the Romans, and found out only some of what had happened to their people as it was happening to them now, too. The Father of Manifestation, who was the reincarnated Head of the Temple at Delphi became a mysterious person who lived deep in the woods and taught only those He thought He could trust and who would keep the knowledge from being lost. His books were in danger of being lost because they were so old by then. Many had not been recopied at the Temple, and even though some Druids helped Him, they were not all copied. When He found some of the Temple people, they all claimed to have escaped because of their own psychic perceptions, but they were working for the Romans. He trusted some of these people to help Him. They changed some of the information in these books, and as keepers of the books, they did not keep them in safe places. And, so it was that that magic and wisdom was lost in the search for power and gold.

LOST WILL NEEDS MORE LIGHT
SOME MORE INFORMATION ON HOW THE GAP MOVED DOWN THROUGH THE CHAKRAS

The Mother's pitiful plight, with every sort of attack and assault going on against Her, not only from My Light, but also Body, Lucifer and most of the other emerged Spirits had made it very difficult for Her to stay alive, let alone be rescued, or even reached by My Loving Light. For a while, I was consumed by the fear that this had gone on for far too long, had gone too far and that My dreams of rescuing the Mother and healing everything were just that…dreams. The role that denial spirits have played made it even more difficult for the Mother because they gave Her only reflections of imprints and judgments they held and no information She could understand without My help.

With the Purple gap in place, it felt, and looked, to Her as though there was no love for Her anywhere. During that time, I sank into Myself over and over, searching within for anything I may have missed that could have told Me anything I didn't already know about how this happened. Always, I was drawn to look at the Mother and Her situation. Over and over, I had to see Her under all sorts of attack. At first, I thought this was just a giant temper tantrum on Her part to get Her way and was very hardened to it. Then, I began to notice a soft place in My Heart for Her that I had sealed over when it looked to Me like She had preferred Body and, then later, Lucifer. I had thought She was aligned with this and was seeking power Herself, but in My Heart, this place was still crying out to know the truth about Her.

Whenever I tried to sink into Myself, lost Will was throwing up such a clamor that I didn't see how I was going to get anywhere this way. I didn't know what this noise was, or what to do about it. If I looked outward, the Mother Warriors tried to get right in My Face to make their point, which I repeatedly missed because of the way they tried to make it. When I turned away from all this, there was Heart, insisting I had to take a closer look. I was overwhelmed, but then, I realized I had to listen to all of it, watch and learn to understand. I began to look more closely at Body's attempts to get rid of the Mother. I saw Him imparting to Her, with His actions, that if She'd just do what He wanted, back off and learn Her place, He wouldn't have to push on Her.

All of this has been difficult for Me to look at, which is why I originally didn't want to look. But, as I have watched everything continue to repeat the original patterns of imbalances over and over and over, and watched Hearts be broken over and over and over, My Own Heart was breaking in pieces, and I did not know how I could help it hold together. This is why I searched the past so diligently. There was no other way My Light knew to try to see where it went so wrong, so tragically and heartbreakingly wrong.

Even the few happy relationships I managed to spot ended in death and separation from their physical manifestation, and even, sometimes, from one another in the astral planes of existence. It all seemed overwhelming to Me, and surely must be to you who have been living it over and over and over.

No matter how big a mess Creation was in, I found that I could not let it go. It must heal, and I found that it can heal. There is no other option, except death. Healing it one tragedy at a time, however, seemed impossibly overwhelming. Then, I found that if Spirits could work their way back to their Original Cause, healing could happen there and heal everything from there forward.

In the gaps I have been describing here, it has been very difficult to look at the Light and see what has really been going on in there, because it has been harsh to blinding, and those looking have felt they could not look into it very well, or for very long. The Light has said it has been because most Spirits cannot handle looking upon the Light of God, but that is not it. In these areas, We did not want what We were really doing there to be seen. We had Our unmoving rage out in front of Us as the protection We thought We needed from a gap We did not, yet, understand or want to look at. This rage preferred to make most Spirits feel pushed back and as though they dared not question the Light of God, but this was not the real Light of God. It was not Loving Light because We were not allowing enough Will presence to have the movement necessary to soften that Light. We perceived that as making openings for inroads We did not want to have. I thought, then, that I preferred to let My unmoved rage keep this gap in place so that I did not have to look at it or even notice it there, but I no longer have this position.

I have already been describing the gap in Purple, the gap between Blue and Purple and Indigo's problems in trying to find its right place between them. There has also been a large gap between the upper and lower chakras, located between Blue and Green that has basically been a gap between Blue and everything else further down. There have also been gaps between all of the Chakras. Green lacked true love, and nature often manifested as brutal and unloving in its behavior. In Yellow, the personal power of love was replaced by the love of power, especially power over others.

Orange's creativity and reproductive powers were judged to be rivalry toward Body, and the lovelessness there impacted Orange's ability to reproduce within love. Red lacked the presence of My Loving Light in its physical manifestation of strength and vitality, and within its instincts for survival. In other words, the Loving Light that should have been flowing abundantly down through the Chakras was in short supply. This can be healed by first finding alignment within the self.

Complicating the situation even more, underneath the presentation being made by Our Main Bodies, slipping down, out and away, were the denials that feared how this unloving light felt and had downright terror of it and how it was being acted out. Often the Will-polarity has felt it can present only compliance and hardly dares even to have its grief there, while also, underneath, embarrassing and terrifying to the rest of the Will, there has been a simmering, smoldering rage that had begun to be increasingly manifest as "other spirits" who were angry at everything, including the rest of the Will, for presenting only acceptance for what unloving light said and did there. These "other spirits" said they knew what was really going on and that the Loving Light was lying about it.

Many of these pieces of unaccepted Will fell into other Chakras and became a lost Will presence that did not harmonize vibrationally with the rest of the Spirits there. This also needs to be sorted out now, and can be done by giving free expression to the Will. The upper Chakras also need to give emotional expression to what they have judged against and not wanted to own as part of themselves in the past. Lost Will has felt it cannot accept the light of unmoved rage, because it feels it and it hurts, but much lost Will has pressured itself to let it be there with them anyway because of what it has had pounded into it by Our denied rage and refusal to look at Ourselves there. We also tried to keep them from looking and seeing it for what it was. Many backed away, only to find that they could not survive without light in some form and have lived very marginal lives, saying they could not understand God. Anger said "the hell with Him," and grief and fear succumbed to believing they must do His bidding anyway.

These areas of the Will have never received Loving Light. They have been in great compression and pain that must end now. When We have felt guilty looking at their lives and were thankful they were not Our lives because We did not want to have to live them, these people have been thought to be guilt reflections. Their lives have been reflections of what they've been holding, but they have not been presenting it, and by now, I think you know why. To find out what they have been holding, they must be felt, and since there has been so much suffocating compression there, this is not likely to be easy. Releasing the judgment that feeling them is only projecting Our own feelings onto them is important, because feeling this is the right approach. These are your own feelings presenting with the judgments you put upon them. Healing this is up to your resolve to do so.

In Purple's gap, it has always looked as though they took spiritual truth and twisted it to make it work for them. It looked as though they held themselves superior, held spiritual truth and light for themselves and their own advantage and didn't share it. In not looking at the way they appeared to be there, Purple allowed everyone else to feel they were unworthy. Within Purple, part of this has been compensation, and part of this has been that they were stopped, backed up and mistreated by Body and couldn't move any farther into Manifestation than they did. Shame and the fear they are inadequate or sexually twisted have been deeply imprinted and denied in Purple. Blue has used this gap to convince Spirits not to be open, or receptive, to Purple, and not to believe it if they did contact anything from My Loving Light, even saying it was the devil instead, but it was the gap saying this.

Blue has tried to make Blue the entire focus of the Spirits on Earth and manipulate this for their own purposes, as though this is all there is to life. Meanwhile, Blue has tried to co-opt and use the lower Chakras however it has seen fit for its own purposes. As long as these gaps have been able to be held in place, this has been true, and the means that have been used to hold them in place have been brutal. The unloving light there has believed that it must not let love prevail, or it was going to be hurt in ways it had already heavily judged it never wanted to have to feel. It was sure it preferred lovelessness to ever having to be hurt, itself, and saw nothing else there, to the extent of not even knowing what it was really doing. No matter how much the conscious mind may present itself as different, unless these imprints are shifted, it will still revert to imprinting when those ancient, unmoved feelings are stirred.

Blue's gap has never looked at the lower Chakras as anything other than something to use for their own benefit and take what it wanted, which has usually been gratification of some sort and orifices for sex. Green was not viewed differently. Even though Blue had to help make Green, Green was treated like a bastard child at the hands of the Blue gap. Green became a tunnel or access road to thrust into the lower Chakras. If Yellow tried to come back up, or vomited, Blue said it was Yellow's fault for resisting what was given to it. If Blue saw Yellow as continuing to resist, Blue would threaten to withhold everything from Yellow and could block the light so Yellow would fear it had no means to survive. Blue's gap didn't care. Blue threatened all the Chakras. The Blue gap has not moved off its position for a long time and needs movement from underneath because it has been sitting on the expression center like the dogs at the gates of hell. Those on the outside have thought the dogs won't let them in, but those inside know the dogs won't let them out. Nonetheless, the up-rush from lost Will is going to happen whether it's allowed and encouraged or forced to erupt like volcanoes, because Orange has been going down fast and Red with it. While the Blue gap has thought it can continue to mine the lower chakras, these colors have been backed down into the feet and, now, the Earth. Blue urgently needs movement in its own held emotional charge around what it has called the surge wars between Blue and Yellow.

There are many other judgments that have also encumbered the flow in and between the Chakras for so long that it is not possible to know what a healthy Chakra system is anymore. For this to change, the Will polarity has to move out what, for so long, has believed deserved this, and as it does, the upper Chakras are going to have to face the reflection of what they have really done there and not push this reflection down and out, denying it its validity again.

All of the lower Chakras have thought and believed that they were unworthy because they were not part of the Godhead, but if they can find their true worth, they'll understand that the Godhead is not Their Right Place. They need color in their lives, and Red, Orange and Yellow, especially, are very colorful and warm Spirits when they are allowed to be. What all the Chakras need is an unimpeded and uncensored flow of My Loving Light passing through the spectrum of their colors to make the glory of Creation. They came forth on a wave of purity in joyful response to this vision in My Loving Light and have been woefully darkened and smudged by Body's co-option of Creation. They have often blamed the Mother for this, but need to look deeper, as I had to.

Many of the Ronalokas have hated the Mother also, for having Them to begin with when They immediately began to feel unaccepted by My Light. They have a strong basis for feeling this way, but no longer need to beg My forgiveness because They have done nothing wrong. They do need to accept, though, that even though I did tell the Father of Manifestation not to have sex with the Mother because of My fears of how We were going to be able to repair the imbalances that had already emerged, let alone handle anymore, the Ronalokas had to emerge there. Even before the Mother was pushed again, She could feel Herself falling. I did not reach for Her there and didn't know, until I really studied Body carefully, why I couldn't. Without being allowed to fully see why this happened to Her, it seemed to the Ronalokas that the Mother had conceived Them in sin, for which They must pay, and just dropped Them out and abandoned Them. I didn't know yet that my own gap had shoved Her out.

The Ronalokas have also had a large amount of lost Will that has fallen into Them from Our denials and have been living out many of them. The Ronalokas already felt motherless when they fell to Earth, and although He was going to find a use for them later, fatherless when the Father of Manifestation's interests soon drew Him elsewhere. The Ronalokas have fear that they are less worthy than others.

When the Ronalokas fell to Earth, they experienced going into compression too fast as the Mother had, and felt terror as the Mother had. They felt pushed by the Father Warriors who had accompanied Them, looming over Them like prison guards, as the Mother had felt forced and pushed by the Father of Manifestation during the emergence of earlier spirits.

On Earth, many Ronalokas polarized to the rage Mother who had been left on Earth. They viewed this part of the Mother as more powerful than the rest of the Mother who had "abandoned" them and not protected or helped them. The rage Mother was not even present when they emerged, but they felt she had been at work, holding a space where they could live after they emerged. The Mother on Earth was telling them exactly that. She told them that without her protective shield, they would be defenseless, but even when they were sexually molested by Satyrs, she did nothing about it. She was afraid of the Satyrs, herself, and wouldn't admit it.

Father Warriors were already hounding the Ronalokas, telling them they needed to be protected from the ruthlessness of Creation by doing their bidding. Even though it looked like the Ronalokas agreed to this, they were really feeling frightened and fatherless since Body didn't come to Earth with them, which they tried to hide. They more succumbed than agreed. Many Ronalokas are still tangled up with Father Warriors, thinking they need their protection and help. Even though there has been rage and terror in the way for a long time, they can open to directly receive My Loving Light now if they want to, and they need to more than many may have realized. Many things the Ronalokas have been holding, densified deep in their bodies, is Will essence that never received light or is Will essence that felt it was hurt by the intensity of the light that first came to it. They have clenched to stop its penetration and have held that light all this time.

HEART ATTEMPTS TO BRIDGE THE GAP IN PURPLE

The Mother was very shut down after Her torture at Delphi, especially in Her third eye. Her next life, after Delphi, was as a slave to some Romans. Her work was in the kitchen and tending the babies. She hovered near their fires to get the chill out of Her bones and warm Her many aches and pains. Even though She came close to them, She still did not like them. She had imprinted that She was nothing but a slave to that kind of light and only as long as She was useful. Her desire to get farther away from Romans managed to vibrate Her to an outer Province for Her next life, but She was not, yet, able to move beyond their reach.

Her self-esteem had gone so low that She was surprised when She found Herself selected to be Mary, the Mother of Jesus. At age twelve, Mary had begun to study with a sect of Judaism called the Essenes. The Essenes believed that love, peace and harmony were the answer to the woes of their world. They thought that a unified Jewish nation with an enlightened ruler could bring these things about and could get rid of the rule of Rome. The Essenes wanted a child to be born with as many bloodlines as possible, thinking this would enable them to unite all the Jews under one King. Many of them had been at Delphi earlier, and once again, most everyone there thought that the right form and more focused light would be successful.

Many pieces of the Mother, as well as many pieces who thought they should be the Mother, were gathering around Mary to bring the largest piece of Heart that they could into manifestation there, and crown him King of all Jews. The Essenes had a ceremony in which they selected Mary to be the mother of this being they were calling into manifestation. This being was going to be as much as could be gathered there of the first Heart Spirit to emerge on the Spirit side in Original Cause. He had imprinted that He was My Only True Son, and although He was a very large piece of this original Spirit, He was lacking much of the Will side of Heart. That night, an Angel announced to Mary that She would soon be giving birth to a son who would go forth and change the world. Mary was not married, or pregnant, and thought it meant that She would soon be married.

That same night, Joseph of Arimathea, who was another incarnation of The Father of Manifestation, and an "uncle" to Mary in the Essenes, came to Her and impregnated Her without entering Her. Although He cared about Her, it was because He also had the "right" bloodlines, and those making these plans did not want to risk anything that would not produce the "right" child. Mary, however, was not allowed to marry Him. The Essenes wanted to keep the identity of this child a secret until the "right" time, and so, a marriage to an older Joseph was arranged. Later, when the Romans decided to deify Jesus, as they did their Emperors, they decided to clean this up by saying it was an immaculate conception.

At the time, however, it was an attempt to put a King on the throne who would be legitimized in ruling over all Jews. Mary was the one to be pregnant and have the baby, but, according to those who made the plan, the rest was going to be in the hands of people considered to be more spiritually enlightened. Mary had already felt shunned by other Essenes and had begun to feel that it was only Her womb that was wanted there because She had the "right" bloodlines and that She was not going to be allowed to raise this child Herself. When Joseph of Arimathea tried to talk to Mary about this, She felt that He was talking down to Her and did not want to listen.

You probably know the story that has been popularized, but I want to make you aware of some other information about Jesus' life. Purple people had arranged to implement this plan. Having been the ones to give the prophecy earlier; along with their healing intent, they also wanted to make themselves right. Jesus was born according to the prophecies that said He would be, and He was born in a stable, largely because the town was full and also because Mary felt excluded everywhere She went. Wise men did come to see Jesus, and one of them said too much to Herod. Mary and Joseph were warned about this, and took the baby Jesus and fled to Egypt. Joseph of Arimathea made His living as a trader and was able to get Them onto a caravan of people He knew who were leaving immediately. Several people, all Essenes, helped Them sneak through houses and back streets to the departure place. Otherwise, it is doubtful Jesus would have survived.

Jesus was schooled at a young age in Egypt by Egyptian Temple people who taught Him many things beyond what was conventionally taught to most people where He was born. He learned about more advanced healing methods and was also introduced to the concepts of magic, ritual, enlightenment and initiation. Among the many things Jesus was taught in Egypt, there were a number of teachings that were not allowed where He was born and that the Romans squelched in their Provinces. When Mary and Joseph decided to return home, Jesus' teachers cautioned Them that Jesus might be targeted because of His knowledge.

When They returned, Jesus was not sent to the Temple. He was sent to the Essenes for His education. When They went to the Temple, Jesus had begun to attract attention to Himself because of the things He was saying, and also because He was shining with light. Joseph of Arimathea told Mary that Jesus was drawing attention from people who could realize He'd been overlooked in Herod's killing of babies. He did not think it was safe for Jesus to stay there anymore until He was old enough to protect Himself. Joseph of Arimathea wanted to take Jesus with Him on a caravan to the East. Mary didn't want Jesus to go away, but knew She had to let Him go for His own safety. Jesus was very excited by the prospect of learning more of the kinds of things He had been taught in Egypt.

Joseph of Arimathea was a spiritual man who sought other spiritual people in His travels. On this trip, Joseph of Arimathea and Jesus spent time in India, Nepal and Tibet where Jesus learned about reincarnation and other methods of meditation and healing. He saw people do some amazing healings, as well as levitate, charm snakes and do other things that amazed Him. Everything seemed very exciting and interesting to Him. He wanted to learn how these things were done. Jesus was a bright student, and He learned well. Even though He was very enthralled with everything He was learning, at times, He wished His mother was there to share it with Him, and talked about this with His "uncle."

As Jesus grew, He began to look more like Joseph of Arimathea than the Joseph He had been told was His father. Joseph of Arimathea saw this and knew it meant He had to keep Jesus away even longer. Jesus had not been told His true identity or His planned destiny, yet, and His "uncle" didn't say anything about being His father. Nonetheless, Jesus began to have feelings that Joseph of Arimathea was His father and did not dare say anything unless His "uncle" said it first.

Because of His vision of bringing people and their cultures together, after a long time in the East, Jesus' "uncle" decided He would take Him to the West. He didn't remember His old connections near the Tor yet, but that is where He was going to go. He told Jesus they would stop in to see His mother, but did not tell Him it would be such a short visit. When They returned, Joseph had died. This was difficult for Jesus even though He had begun to think Joseph of Arimathea was His real father. Mary was very grieved and also lonely for Jesus. She was sitting on their flat roof when She saw them coming toward Her. At first, She didn't believe Her eyes, and thought Her tears had deceived Her. When She realized it really was Them, She was very excited to see Them, but Their resemblance to each other was so startling that She also felt uneasy. She hurriedly came down to meet Them, and before She could even embrace Jesus, Joseph wanted to get inside because He also knew the dangers of Their close resemblance.

Jesus sat with Mary and held Her as comfort for Their grief over the loss of His "father." Several Essenes came to the house that night as though they somehow knew Joseph and Jesus were there. When it came time to go to bed, Joseph told Mary that They needed to leave very early in the morning to catch another caravan, to the West this time, as He knew He must keep Jesus away until the right time. As Jesus' "uncle" it did not seem unusual, especially now that His "father" was gone, that Joseph of Arimathea would take Jesus along with Him and teach Him His livelihood. Mary had some anger and bitterness, then, that She had been used to have this child She loved so much and couldn't have near Her, but kept it to Herself.

In the West, near the site of the old Temple, Jesus was taught many more things. Many things they were teaching Him were not very different from what He had learned in the East, and He also showed them some things He had learned in the East. Jesus thought that people so far away from one another, yet having so many of the same things to teach meant that these teachings must be right, and when He applied them, they seemed to work. Jesus was fascinated by stories he was reading of the distant past, but they didn't go back far enough for Him to understand why some people were favored with healings and others were not, and neither had I. We were still thinking We could let bygones be bygones. Imprinting was not known of then, and Jesus had embraced the idea of Karma and thought that explained it for Him.

While Jesus was on His distant travels, He was growing into a young man broadened by travel and study. He still missed His mother at times, but the longer He was away, the more Her presence was receding in His consciousness. When Jesus came back to Her after being so far away for so long, Mary did not like feeling that He was acting subtly aloof and superior toward Her, especially in spiritual knowing. When Jesus showed His love for Her, it had begun to feel rather patronizing to Her. Mary felt quite heartbroken about Her relationship with Her firstborn child, but tried to overlook it.

As Jesus began to teach and demonstrate what He had learned in other places, many young women began to cluster around Him whenever He appeared anywhere. His lack of Will presence wasn't solved by the presence of these Heart daughters, but it helped Him to feel grounded and to remain on Earth. He needed His own Will which had been pushed away so long ago that He didn't realize it was missing. Mary had previously been the one to ground Jesus. She was feeling increasingly moved to the fringe and had begun to worry that Jesus' public conduct did not look good to certain sects in the Temple. Mary wanted Joseph of Arimathea to encourage Jesus to select one of these young women as His wife. The Essenes and Joseph of Arimathea wanted Jesus to solidify His position for the throne through marriage to the right woman with the right bloodlines, but Jesus had other ideas. He was full of what He had learned and had begun to teach and heal.

Jesus showed no bias regarding social class, sex or age. This was immediately viewed as a threat by those who wanted to maintain the status quo. That he would touch lepers and other diseased people outraged certain sects of Jews who had been maintaining almost a caste system similar to what Jesus had witnessed in India. That He would do healings and perform miracles on the Sabbath further outraged certain Jews. He was doing many miraculous healings, often just because of the presence of My Loving Light in Him. That He would help anyone who would receive Him, free of charge, also further outraged people who had power positions in the Temple and charged money for their services, sometimes a lot of money. Jesus said that Jehovah was not discriminatory, so He could not be. Jesus was so radiant with Light and miraculously helped so many people that many people began to think He was Jehovah come to Earth. When they tried to say He was Jehovah, Jesus said He was the son of Jehovah.

Mary felt the dangers of what Jesus was doing, and asked Joseph of Arimathea to speak to Jesus about it. Joseph of Arimathea was angry when He cautioned Jesus, and Jesus' anger answered Joseph by saying the Father He answered to was in Heaven. Joseph of Arimathea's anger felt disregarded by this. He thought Jesus was making too much of a public stir and too many claims too quickly instead of going to those who would want the opportunity to recognize Him before, not after, the people did. Joseph of Arimathea thought He had the connections to help Jesus gain the throne that they wanted Him to have there. Jesus didn't want to do what Joseph of Arimathea wanted Him to do. Joseph wanted Jesus to gain the throne before He showed people what He could do. Jesus saw that these people were too narrow-minded to be pleased by anything He did. He told Joseph of Arimathea that He wanted to keep doing what He was doing until the people demanded He be put on the throne.

Jesus continued to speak publicly and did many healings, some of them through simple health practices the people didn't know about and some of them truly miracles in terms of what Loving Light can do. Even though Jesus told people they could learn to do such things themselves, Jesus was so advanced in His ability to receive and shine light, that most of the people, who were lost Will, saw these healings as miracles they could not imagine themselves able to do. Many of them attached themselves to Jesus as pieces of His own lost Will. As word spread of Jesus' miraculous healings, crowds grew larger wherever He appeared. A number of people, including a number of the young Heart women, began to move around with Jesus as a kind of following. This was a freedom that was not accorded to unmarried women there, and the Pharisees, and others, began to say these young women were prostitutes. Joseph of Arimathea insisted that Jesus get married.

Even though Jesus did marry Mary Magdalene, and She did have the bloodlines the Essenes wanted Him to marry, there was now a problem of reputation. Jesus refused to be married in the Temple, and the Pharisees, the Sanhedrim and the Sadducees said the Essene marriage wasn't valid because it didn't take place in the Temple. Jesus disregarded their opinions.

While Jesus thought he was gaining popular momentum, as his popularity grew, those in power increasingly viewed Him as a threat. By now, they had realized that Jesus could proclaim Himself King of the Jews, and had decided they must get rid of Him. To do this, they decided to discredit Him first. The Pharisees, and others, continued to claim that the women around Jesus were all prostitutes and produced a growing list of charges against Jesus including blasphemy, the breaking of the Sabbath, interfering with justice by saving adulterous women and other crimes against Jewish law. When the Romans heard that Jesus could be the rightful King of the Jews, they began to accuse Him of inciting rebellion against Rome.

Jesus' activities had alarmed Mary, Joseph of Arimathea and the other Essenes, who were all already viewed as too liberal by many other Jewish sects. They knew these Jews could try to stop Jesus before He gained the throne and would have the power to overrule them. Jesus had already stirred a desire for revenge when He turned over the tables of the money changers in the Temple. When the Pharisees began to say that Jesus' healings were coming from Beelzebub, the Essenes, as well as Mary and Joseph of Arimathea, knew that influential Jews would try to have Jesus killed.

Jesus told Joseph of Arimathea that He no longer wanted to be an earthly King and that His realm was not an earthly realm. Jesus was listening to His parents, but not heeding Their warnings. Joseph asked Jesus to go away for a while, but it was already too late. Even though Jesus did withdraw at times, He didn't really believe anything could happen to Him. He thought He was totally protected by My Light. Jesus had decided He had a mission to bring spiritual truth to the people and could not be held back. I helped Jesus with My Loving Light as much as I could, but the gap in Purple was a very real problem.

Joseph of Arimathea had been growing increasingly exasperated with Jesus for not listening to Him, but He did love Him as His son. Mary pleaded with Joseph to save Jesus. She wanted Joseph to take Jesus out of the country quickly, but Jesus would not go. Joseph then went to men in power, both Roman and Jewish, with whom He had influence. He used His influence to make a deal, but it was not the deal He wanted to make to have Jesus put on the throne. They all still wanted to have Jesus arrested and questioned. The Romans wanted to crucify him. Pilate saw public opinion as demanding He have Jesus flogged. The Jews wanted to have Jesus stoned. Although He wasn't going to say it, Joseph thought Jesus' chances of surviving would be better if He was crucified. He told them it was likely a mob would arise and fight them if they tried to stone Jesus. Thinking many of Jesus' followers would be there, Joseph of Arimathea tried to have these men agree to let Jesus test His popularity by asking the public what His fate should be. He wasn't able to prevail with anyone there. Jesus had publicly outraged them too many times.

When Jesus knew of His impending plight, He thought that His spiritual knowledge would enable Him to transcend His situation. At the last supper He had with His closest followers, He told them as much. He did some ceremonial things there, including having His followers drink from a shared chalice, later known as the Holy Grail, saying the wine was His blood, and the bread He was breaking was

His body. He made a covenant with them to continue the work that He had begun. Jesus' disciples were parts of His own lost Will, and without Jesus as Their cohesive center, they weren't able to move along very far.

Simon, or Peter, had Jesus' denied fears of competition and jealousy over His position as first born. The Peter who denied Jesus had another aspect of Jesus' denied fears of what could result from competition, jealousy and rivalry if Jesus showed Himself as anything more than all the others. Bartholomew, or Nathaniel, and Thaddeus, or Jude, had denied imprints in which Jesus had accused Himself of self-aggrandizement. James, the great, and James, the less, as well as Andrew and John had denied self-love that Jesus had pushed away with the fear that He thought too much of Himself. Thomas had Jesus' denied self-doubt. When Judas Iscariot went to betray Jesus' whereabouts, Jesus knew it was going to happen because Judas was the one who had not trusted Him. Judas had Jesus' denied lack of trust in Himself. Judas' behavior toward Jesus reflected Original Cause imprints that Jesus had taken in as the Father of Manifestation's real intent toward Him. The denials Jesus had pushed out even further, acted to bring Him down and try to kill Him. While the drama was about to intensify in Jesus' life, the real healing that must come now is the inner healing.

When the Romans arrested Jesus, Pilate and Herod were curious about what Jesus was going to say to them. They passed him back and forth, trying to decide what to do with Him. Jesus was not giving them the answers they wanted, and Pilate had begun to think that they were being played with. Furious, he had Jesus flogged to "soften Him up for questioning." The Roman soldiers there ridiculed, belittled and made fun of Jesus, giving Him a bitter crowning as King of the Jews when they put the crown of thorns on His head. Jesus began to feel the seriousness of His situation then. Finally, Jesus was told it had been decided to let the people decide His fate. When Jesus was brought to the public place where His fate was going to be decided, His followers were barely present. The crowd was stacked with Romans, Roman sympathizers, and the Jewish sects who had opposed Jesus. When they were asked if Jesus should be released, the crowd demanded that another be released instead. Jesus was shaken by this.

In His weakened state, He was forced to carry the cross on which He would be crucified. Many tried to help Jesus along the way, but only the lowliest amongst them was allowed to. Joseph of Arimathea had tried to get Jesus crucified on His private land. He had told Jesus to feign death as soon as He could if they decided to kill Him, and He would get Him taken down from the cross. Jesus was an adept who knew how to stop His heart and His breathing. Joseph thought that if Jesus was not dead, they could still help Him and manage to get Him out of the country. Jesus felt that even if He was dead, He could overcome it. The Romans suspected something and sent some Roman soldiers to guard the Crucifixion, saying it was for security.

On the day of the Crucifixion, My emotions over another failed attempt to bridge the gap Purple had with the rest of Manifestation darkened the skies along with everyone else's emotions. Jesus still believed He was going to have the power to transmute the situation. The outer situation needed to be transformed by inner movement and shifts, but outer was still the focus there. Jesus used everything He knew to survive His ordeal on the Cross as if it was an initiation, but at times, His pain was greater than His spiritual teachings had prepared Him for, and He revealed His "humanness," much to the gratification of some of the Roman soldiers there who had been enjoying ridiculing Him.

When Jesus was laid to rest in Joseph of Arimathea's own planned burial shrine, He was in a deep coma-like meditation. He was not breathing and had stopped His heart. He was anointed with aloe, myrrh and other healing herbs they knew and wrapped in herbal poultices. I helped Him as much as I could. Jesus' followers also helped Him by meditating and focusing as much light on Him as they could. The sword wound Jesus had received at the last minute from a soldier who, they thought, was perhaps trying to end Jesus' suffering, was most grievous. In the "tomb," Jesus was also working on His own healing. The women closest to the "tomb" fell asleep focusing on Him and did not see Jesus arise or how the large stone at the doorway was moved.

The healing and "resurrection" of Jesus there, in such a short time, was miraculous to those who had not studied what Jesus had learned. Even so, it was amazing, especially given His circumstances. Most people haven't, yet, been able to accomplish the immensity of such a healing, but the doorway to this healing does not need to be torture, pain and suffering. Even though Jesus was amazingly healed in three days, it still took some time before He was strong enough to leave. Initially, Jesus was still very pale from blood loss, but He was determined to let some of the people He was closest to see Him before He left, and even let them touch His hands to be sure it was really Him. At times, He was barely physical because He was undecided as to whether He wanted to leave Earth or not. He still felt attached to some of the people He had known, especially His mother, wife and child. Joseph felt that because of the appearances Jesus had made, He had to move Jesus from place to place to keep Him from being arrested again. Because of these appearances, Joseph of Arimathea also realized Jesus was also going to have to leave. He told Himself He would go to the East with Jesus where the Roman's were not in control.

Jesus wanted His wife and their child to go with Him. When Mary Magdalene, who was pregnant, refused to go to such a strange, faraway and unknown to her place, They realized that She, also, could not stay there and could not travel alone. She did not tell Jesus there was another child on the way. Joseph decided He would have to take Her and their child and go West by sea, which felt familiar to Her as it almost retraced the route She had taken in the earlier Delphi life. She was afraid to go to the East, but it was also Her unmoved rage at what She had just been put through that carried Her away to the West with Joseph of Arimathea. Mary Magdalene ended their journey in the South of Gaul when she couldn't travel anymore in her state. They reached the Isle only later. Jesus was very disturbed by this turn of events, but knew He had to go East.

In case She would not go with them, Joseph of Arimathea did not want to let Mary know where any of them were going to go, but he offered to take Her along. Mary was in great grief, and also felt unwelcome again for reasons She could not explain. She said only that She had the other children, so no. Mary stayed behind to see the persecution of Her son's followers begin, and feelings of bitterness about the whole situation arose again. When She could stand no more, She turned Her face to the wall and died in a bitterness that took a long time to recede. She wanted the love of Heart to be enough, as I did, as We all did, but without the Will side, it was not enough.

When Jesus had begun His ministry, lower Chakra people seemed to like His message and His presence, but Blue's imprints saw this as a threat to their position at the top. Even though Jesus did not, yet, realize it, Purple was about to be cut out of the picture again, and thus, My true message was aborted there. After Jesus' "death," Christians were persecuted. Later, when the Romans decided to use the rising popularity of Christianity to try to hold their Empire together, they deified Jesus, as they did their Emperors, but when Jesus was alive, they cast Him down and imprinted His followers, again, that the messages from Purple were not real. They have edited these messages similarly to the way the books were edited at Glastonbury. Even though it appeared that the presence then known as the Father of Manifestation had tried to help the situation, once again, he stepped away at crucial moments, and his denials retained the power position on Earth. Lower Chakra people were still defined as the lowly sinners who had displeased God and must forever slave, serve and beg forgiveness while those who had been imprinted by the Father of Manifestation's denied rage in Blue maintained their position at the top and gave themselves the most of everything. In effect, the message was: If you receive God's Light and try to bring His true messages forth, you will be killed.

KING ARTHUR

I have another story to tell that is involved in the splits We have been trying to heal.

In the times preceding King Arthur, the Romans had given up on finding the gold they had heard about, and on finding the Holy Grail. They disliked the climate and found the people to be unruly and unable or unwilling to pay taxes to Rome. They withdrew from the British Isles, giving no warning or leadership in transition. In this time period, there was much struggle for the rulership of the British Isles, with various Lords of the Land, all Father of Manifestation pieces who had issues with one another and were vying for and claiming the right to be King. Many of these people had cooperated with the Romans and were not popular with the people.

Merlin was a Spirit-polarized piece of Heart and a Druid who took pride in his knowledge of magic. He had not seen Himself as welcome in the Purple, Jesus scenario and had been incarnating on the Isle, then known as Avalon, feeling there was magic there. He saw what was happening when the Romans departed and watched with angst as the Lords of the Land fought about who was going to have the position of King and rule over the others. They had great distrust, treachery and intrigue among them. Merlin did not realize what he was seeing in these terms then, but he did firmly believe that their problem was a lack of Heart presence. Merlin had his own rage and many judgments against it. He wanted to be loving and reasonable and appeal to them from the wisdom he felt he had there. Without his own rage in motion there, Merlin could not understand the depth or intensity of this rage or see that it had no interest in being reasonable, and especially not reasonable according to Heart.

Merlin, then, decided he needed to invoke some greater power they would listen to and began to present his teachings as surrounded and supported by signs and omens, mystical teachings and prophecies and anything else he thought would help support the position he wanted others to take there. Merlin was already a mysterious person of undetermined origin and age, and he decided it would be helpful to enhance his reputation. When he wanted to give an understanding that required reincarnational memory that others didn't have there, he simply said he was alive then, and told them what he wanted them to know about it. When something didn't sound quite right to others according to the point of view they wanted to have, he would point to the heavens and say it was right there to be read by those who could and start giving them lessons about the stars they did not really want to have until they said, "Whatever you say."

Merlin took this literally, but they were laughing at him behind his back until some of his predictions came true, some of his omens came to pass and some bad things happened to some people that he had said would happen if they didn't change their ways. Merlin decided that he wanted to arrange to have a child born who would have the right bloodlines to be able to deserve the throne and unite the kingdom again. This child was the Father of Manifestation getting born again into a place with which he was familiar.

Merlin wanted this person to have more Heart presence and planned to be his teacher. Merlin did not mind manipulating Arthur's parentage to accomplish this, and planned to hide him and have him raised by others to keep him safe until it was the right time. It was Igraine who had given birth to Arthur and had given him up, both to protect him and because she didn't want to believe that her own husband had been killed in battle. She thought he would come back one day and find that she had had a child while he was away. Merlin had given her a drugged potion that had caused her to hallucinate the return of her husband and she had had sex with the man who had come to her in her drugged state.

Her older child, Morgaine, was sleeping in the same room and was not drugged. This man had not seemed to know her and had said nothing to her. Morgaine saw that this man was not her father, but she could not talk yet, and only cried when he got in bed with her mother, had sex with her and departed without a word. This man had been sent by Merlin. Later, when he came to claim her mother's hand in marriage, Morgaine felt a rancor toward him. He did not dare mention that he had been the one who had come to Igraine that night, but when he asked if she had another child, Morgaine felt that he must have been the one and her rancor toward him became one of feeling that he had had her father killed. Igraine would not say that she had had another child, but Morgaine felt, then, that she wanted to avenge her father's death through her brother, Arthur.

Many times Merlin went to the family where he had placed Arthur in order to educate him in the ways he wanted him educated. Merlin tried to include other children in that family, but none of them were very interested in or had talent for what Merlin was teaching. Arthur was rather brilliant, but had His own ideas that did not always agree with Merlin. Whenever they disagreed, I later saw, it was because they had touched into an area where old imprints were held. Merlin would feel that they had a stand-off, but he persisted, hoping the lad would see his point of view as time went on.

Arthur had no idea who Merlin considered Him to be until the day came when Merlin revealed that He was claimant to the throne of the King and had the bloodlines that should rule over all of the other Lords who were fighting to gain that power. Arthur looked at His family and didn't know how that could be. Then, Merlin told Him who His real parents were. Arthur hardly knew what to say or do. He had grown to love this family. Suddenly, He felt overwhelmed by how much fighting He knew there was, and how many powerful looking Lords He had heard about who were doing the fighting. He felt He had become a man, but now, He suddenly felt like a boy again.

Arthur and His "family" were all going to go to a tournament, but now, Arthur wasn't sure He wanted to go. He knew Merlin was planning to go and was afraid of what Merlin might say or do. Arthur, however, didn't want to tell His "family" why He suddenly didn't want to go. They knew He had been looking forward to it as an opportunity to test His prowess with the sword. Merlin was already there when Arthur and His "family" arrived, but let only Arthur see Him. Merlin had carefully placed a sword he said he had gotten from "the Lady of the Lake" for Arthur in a large, nearby stone. The sword in the stone attracted great curiosity. Many tried to pull it out of the stone, but none could.

During the tournament, an opponent hit Arthur's sword out of his hand, and it broke on the ground. Arthur's brother had seen the sword in the stone, and when Arthur asked him to quickly get him another sword, his brother decided the sword in the stone was the closest one. He tried to grab it, but could not. He called Arthur to try. Arthur had a great focus of unpremeditated urgency when he tried to pull the sword from the stone, and Merlin was standing nearby to focus the power of His intent. When Arthur tried, He was able to pull the sword from the stone.

Merlin suddenly appeared then, and said that since Arthur had pulled the sword from the stone and the others had not, this made Him King. Suddenly, everyone was arguing about why this should make Him King since He didn't have any of the bloodlines that would qualify Him to be their King. When Merlin revealed Arthur's parentage, even His "family" didn't know. Everyone, then, began arguing about if this was possible, how old Arthur could be, having a boy for a King and when His parents had married. Merlin knew this was a weak point in his plan, but felt He had to do it when the stars were right. Arthur was seeing that He was still going to have to fight for His kingdom.

Arthur felt quite overwhelmed, but felt that any display of emotion would only make Him look even more weak and unprepared in their eyes. Arthur wasn't even sure He wanted to be a King, and least of all, a King who had to fight for his kingdom. Arthur's "father" clearly couldn't show favoritism toward Arthur, since His "brother" now seemed to be a little jealous. Arthur suddenly felt dependent upon Merlin for His claim, His identity and as His only ally there; Merlin, who He was at odds with so much of the time!

Arthur did not know what He was going to be able to do about all of these powerful Lords who seemed to want to protest His claim to the throne. When Merlin took Him aside and assured Him that His sword was named Excalibur, and with it, He could not be defeated, it hardly sank in. Arthur was thinking about the "family" He had lived with all of these years and what that meant now. Soon, Merlin was urging him to give a speech, but Arthur hardly knew what to say and only mumbled something about hoping He could be a good King. The crowd wanted more, and Arthur found there were some things He could say about wanting fair rule and council meetings. The crowd was elated to think that someone had appeared who could end the fighting and restore peace, even if He was a boy, but the Lords who had been doing the fighting weren't so pleased. They wanted to continue the arguments, and the fighting, but Merlin countered each argument on Arthur's behalf. When Arthur went on to win the tournament, they let their arguments subside for the time being.

There were still many obstacles to being crowned King, but Merlin presided over all of them, and eventually, Arthur was crowned King. Arthur still found, though, that many of those who opposed Him would not come to the council meetings He said He was going to have. They didn't want to participate in policy discussions; they wanted to have things the way they wanted to have them, whether it was just or not. They told Arthur to have His decisions delivered to them and often, they refused to receive the knights Arthur sent. When they did receive His knights, Arthur often found out later that these Lords had found ways to misinterpret the decisions, sometimes by sending a message back that Arthur had to send formal decrees. Besides having many knights patrolling His kingdom, sometimes Arthur had to do the fighting Himself. Opposing Lords and some of their loyal knights were the source of much of the fighting Arthur and His knights were having to do to gain control of Arthur's kingdom and bring, at least, the outer appearance of peace.

Without consciously knowing what He was trying to do, Arthur was seeking to deal with His fragmentation, but only outwardly, not inwardly. The ones who were more rage-polarized and turned against him didn't want to cooperate. These had been some of the Centaurs who had sprung forth when He set foot in Pan as a Pegasus. Arthur became exasperated with them and gave the places at His council meetings to Heart pieces who agreed with Him instead. The alignment He was able to find became His Knights of the Round Table, but Merlin set himself apart as Arthur's personal advisor and did not sit there.

Many of the defeated Lords stopped opposing openly, as though they were tired of fighting, but Arthur knew this was not a real allegiance and thought they were just becoming more secretive about their opposition. He was becoming a very popular king with those who were experiencing the benefits of His rule, and thought He could hold onto His kingdom through His popularity.

Arthur still had not married. He wanted to marry for love. Merlin strongly felt He needed to find someone He could love who also belonged to the right family to solidify His hold on the Kingdom. Merlin had someone in mind, who was the daughter of an opposing Lord, but Arthur didn't like this woman as much as He liked Guinevere, daughter of a Lord who had almost the right bloodlines. Merlin gave the marriage his blessing, even though he felt uneasy about it. He knew that opposing Arthur would cause Arthur to oppose him more.

Arthur was enamored of Guinevere's soft sweetness there, and in less than a year's time, they were married. There were some years of peace and prosperity in the kingdom, then, during which Arthur thought Guinevere had blessed his kingdom with good fortune. When Arthur and Guinevere had enough good years together to build Camelot along with the Knights of the Round Table and their entourage in court, and live the lives of peace, happiness and abundance in the land upon which the legends were based, Arthur thought Merlin had been wrong. After some years, however, there was still no heir. Guinevere was a Purple daughter who was not able to have children, and Morgaine saw this as her opportunity to do to Arthur what had been done to her mother.

Arthur felt He had grown up a lot as King, but His guilt had made the Round Table egalitarian. Arthur then found that He didn't feel safe giving all of the information to everyone there, especially since some had alliances with families who still directly opposed Him, yet, it did not seem possible to give privileged information only to some, and so, some had less information than they really should have had, and some had more information than they really should have had. Since they all had an equal say in matters, this gave Him some problems making policies the way He wanted them to be. When it came to the opposing Lords, Arthur thought He could turn things in His own favor if, instead of looking to the opposing Lords, He went out into the countryside and let the people get to know Him rather than continue to think that the policies they didn't like were coming from Him. This further agitated the opposing Lords who began again to actively seek His downfall.

Arthur began to think that traveling around the land talking to the local people was not turning out to be as helpful as He had hoped. He began to question who His allies really were. He felt that He was not going to be able to rule His land if He did not get the people's support somehow, and He did not know how to do this when there were local Lords constantly troubling the people with policies they said were the King's policies when they were not. He decided to try to accomplish the same thing with the festivals and tournaments that would get people to come together outside of their own local area and see that it was not the same everywhere. Then, they might see that some Lords actually followed the King's policies and that the people were happier and better off in those places.

It was to one of these festivals that Morgaine, who did not generally feel welcome in Arthur's court, came and was invited to dinner. There, there was much activity in the great hall, and Morgaine found the opportunity to put something in Arthur's drink. She had studied with Merlin, and this was the potion Merlin had given her mother the night of Arthur's conception. When she saw Arthur excuse himself from the table, she surreptitiously followed him. When He went to His bed chamber, she slipped past the guard and entered His bed chamber pretending to be Guinevere. Arthur, unknowingly, had sex with His half-sister, and she, having consulted the stars herself, conceived His soon-to-be son.

By this time, Arthur and Guinevere were not loving each other the way Arthur thought they were in the beginning. He was very happy that she had come to Him that night as she hadn't seemed to share His interest in having sex. When He thanked her in the morning, she didn't seem to know anything about it. He told Himself she must have had too much Meade like He did.

Arthur began to feel sick after that because Morgaine had also poisoned Him so that it wouldn't be immediately fatal, but would cause Him to waste away. Guinevere had told Arthur she loved Lancelot, and Arthur thought He was growing sick with heartache. Merlin didn't like the partying at Arthur's court, and so, wasn't present or he would have known what happened and could, perhaps, have prevented it or known how to reverse it. It seemed to Arthur that all the love and happiness had been drained from His life. He felt dismal and hopeless most of the time. He seldom rose from His bed.

Guinevere was torturing herself with guilt and fear that she was wrong to love Lancelot, and began taking herself farther and farther into Christianity or, more specifically, the Roman Catholic Church. This disturbed Arthur, who had

had a Celtic upbringing. The Catholic Church was bringing forward His old imprints about God. Arthur thought that I had found a way to punish Him. Guinevere was talking to Him about begging forgiveness. Arthur didn't really want to listen, but when she told Him about the cup used by Jesus at the last supper, He let her say more. He suddenly felt a strong connection to it, and began to think that finding it was going to be His salvation. He felt sure that Joseph of Arimathea had brought this cup to His land not so long ago.

Arthur began sending Lancelot out in search of this chalice, by then thought to be the Holy Grail. When Lancelot didn't find it, Arthur began sending out other knights on a quest to find it, but they were looking far away, some even going to the south of Gaul. Arthur hadn't remembered that He was Joseph of Arimathea, or where He had put this chalice, but He felt it was nearby, hidden someplace, but He didn't know where.

There was still no heir, and Arthur still thought it was the meade they'd had at dinner that night that had caused Guinevere to have sex with Him, but she wouldn't drink with Him anymore. Now, she only drank wine for Holy Communion and begged Him to take Communion. Finally, He told her to have Communion brought to Him, but, then, when Guinevere did agree to have sex with Him, there was still no heir. Soon, Arthur began to hear that Morgaine, who now called herself Morgan le Fey, had a son. Since He had no heir, this was threatening to Arthur.

Arthur did not like his half-sister and feared that this son might, somehow, have the bloodlines that could take over the throne. He feared she had aligned herself with some powerful Lord who opposed Him, and felt urgent to know the age of this son. When he learned it, he began to wonder and fear whether He might be the father of a son conceived with his half-sister. Morgaine said she was keeping who the father was a secret until the right time.

Morgaine had been so sweet to Arthur that night, He had thought it was Guinevere. He even felt some guilt that He had misjudged his half-sister and been too harsh toward her. Having the parents he had, he had taken in kindness as love and wasn't seeing the guile behind much of it. Arthur was hungry for love and didn't know that Morgaine had put a sleeping potion in Guinevere's drink that night and had helped her ever so "kindly" to bed, sitting with her until she was deeply asleep. Arthur had been longing for Guinevere so much that night that he had hallucinated her face when Morgaine had slipped into bed with Him.

Merlin did not agree that there was anything sweet about Morgaine. "As long as she gets what she wants," Merlin had said. "If she doesn't, then you'll see how unsweet she is," but Arthur had begun to have trouble seeing that. Merlin had begun to tell Arthur that he had determined, by divination, what happened to Him that night. Arthur didn't want to hear His worst fears confirmed and asked Merlin, angrily, why he didn't divine it before it was too late. Merlin only said, "I have tried and tried to warn you."

Arthur was suffering so much that He began to have fears that He was going to lose His mind. Merlin tried to remedy the devastating effects of the potion Morgaine had given him, and had some success. The rest, he said, was the result of Arthur's own anguish of heart. Then, Guinevere told Him she had remembered that it was Morgaine who had helped her to her bed that night when she had had too much to drink. Arthur knew, now, what had happened, or feared that He did. He left Guinevere in a frightened rage and rode all of the way to Morgaine's without stopping that night. When he arrived, he insisted on seeing her and demanded to know who the father of her child was. When she would not tell Him, He demanded to see the child. She told Him He would have to wait until morning.

When Arthur saw the boy, he was just of the age he would have been if it had been her that night, and Arthur told Morgaine he suspected her of this.

"And if it were to be true?" she said. "What are you going to do about it now, Arthur? Ah, sweet, guileless Arthur." She was facing away from Him when she said this and turned toward Him suddenly, startling Him because she looked so evil to Him. "You had it coming, Arthur! Oh, how you had it coming! Now the tables are turned! Now it's my son who has the bloodlines to gain the throne!"

Arthur got on His horse and rode away, feeling His whole world was tumbling down around Him. He had been trying to create a heaven on Earth in Camelot. It was His goal in uniting the kingdom, in trying to bring peace, in building Camelot and in everything else He had done or tried to do, and now, He felt it all falling apart.

Facing the long ride back with a tired horse, He rode as slowly as He dared, not knowing if Morgaine had sent anyone in pursuit of Him. He was in a daze and hadn't asked for any food or water from Morgaine because He was still suffering from the effects of what she had given Him before and didn't trust her. His horse was hungry and thirsty and kept stopping to graze. When Arthur urged him on, his horse didn't like it. When they entered the woods they had to pass through, the horse tried to look for water. Sitting on him, Arthur was not paying attention and was badly scratched with branches and brambles. He had not paid attention to where the path was. Arthur and his horse became lost in the woods. Arthur was in such a state, He began to think he was going to the house in the woods where He had grown up.

Eventually, they found a path, but Arthur did not know where it went. He didn't know if He was in friendly terrain or not. He needed to see the sun, but the forest was thick and dark. That night, Arthur didn't sleep well. He had nothing with Him to comfort Him from the cold. In the morning, He felt the sun had risen in the direction He was headed away from, and managed to find His way home at last. When He arrived, He was almost unrecognizable as the King. Arthur was helped to His chambers and never fully recovered. He feared Morgaine had somehow been able to do something else to him, and wondered what age she thought her son had to be to take the throne away from Him. As time went on, and He was not recovering, He called His knights to Him over and over, asking them to continue their search for the Holy Grail.

Merlin was watching all of this, and feeling less and less received by Arthur when He tried to advise Him about anything. Merlin covered His disappointment with anger, and one day, He told Arthur He was going away and might not return. Arthur did not know if this meant Merlin was going to die, or what it meant, but it gave Him another feeling of abandonment. Arthur hadn't always agreed with Merlin, but He didn't like it when Merlin wasn't there to talk to whether He followed his advice or not. When Arthur asked Merlin not to leave, Merlin said, "What do you need me for, you don't listen to me?"

In addition to His many other woes, Arthur was increasingly disturbed to see the growing influence of Christianity around Him beginning to persecute their Celtic ways, shunning Earthly existence and the Body and calling all of the pleasures they had previously enjoyed as natural and a celebration of physical existence, sin. Guinevere removed herself to a convent. Arthur began to withdraw His essence from that lifetime and to wither, at a rather young age, into an old man hardened with the anger that everyone else had done this to Him.

Arthur was continuing to hear increasing bad news of Morgaine's mounting threat from the East and of his son's bad attitude toward Him. Arthur felt sure Morgaine had poisoned Mordred's attitude toward Him. In His delirium, Arthur hoped it wasn't irreparable, and one day, He set out to find him. Several of His loyal knights insisted on going with Him. When Arthur found Mordred, Mordred would not talk to Him. Instead, he attacked Arthur. In His weakened state, Arthur could not fend him off, and Mordred stabbed Him with His own sword, Excalibur.

The knights who were with Arthur surrounded His body to defend Him, thinking He was dead. When they found that Arthur was wounded and not dead, they said nothing. They laid Arthur across His horse as though He was dead so that Mordred would not follow, and took Him to a place where they thought Merlin might be. Merlin was not there, but there were others there who tried to heal

Arthur. Arthur's heart for living was gone, however, and He gave up on His life there.

Mordred was not taken seriously as a possibility for King. He was declared illegitimate by the standards of the new religion, the Roman Catholic Church, which Morgan le Fey refused to recognize. Morgaine had wanted Mordred to save the old ways for her, but the old ways could not be saved there. The Church opposed the Celtic ways and the Druids as well. Instead of being able to build a bridge between the two worlds, the gap that was holding them apart, once again, held its power position, and the Dark Ages that had gripped Europe descended upon the Isle.

MERLIN AND MORGAN LE FEY

When Merlin left Arthur, he went to Morgan Le Fey and tried to convince her to ally with Arthur instead of displacing Him. Morgan Le Fey would not hear of it. She, in fact, resented Merlin for putting Arthur on the throne when she thought it could have been her. Merlin, by then, had a deep resentment, himself, toward Arthur for not solidifying His kingdom through marriage and for, so often, not listening to him.

Over and over, Morgan Le Fey was practicing her magical arts. She talked to the ethers, forming her plan and drawing to her any energy that would be in alliance with her plan. She was talking to her rage-polarized lost Will that was in opposition to Arthur having the power position He had. She also had ears at the Castle and especially did not want to hear that Guinevere was pregnant. Potions were delivered to the Castle and given to Guinevere to drink without her knowing that they prevented or caused miscarriage of pregnancy. When the opportunity came to disgrace Arthur through Lancelot's relationship with Guinevere, Morgan Le Fey spread this information far and wide. Then, she felt, if an heir were ever produced, it would be easy to cast doubt on the parentage.

Morgan Le Fey found herself drawing Lords who opposed Arthur. They all pressed themselves on her, wanting to have sex with her. She told them all, "If you help me take Arthur from His throne, you can have me sexually."

Morgan Le Fey did not tell any of them who Mordred's father really was. There were many years to wait while Mordred grew up. It was not easy to keep her allies together for that time, but she continually reminded them that they had a mission and a purpose for remaining allies there. She also kept them in a sexual frenzy of sorts by giving them potions of hallucinogenics and aphrodisiacs and telling them, when they had sex, that her sexuality was the most powerful.

When Morgan Le Fey saw that Mordred might not be powerful enough on his own, she wanted to find someone to help them. When Merlin came, Morgan Le Fey decided that if she established a bond with Merlin, he would put her son on the throne the way he had Arthur. Merlin had bloodlines she liked; they were Celtic. Morgan Le Fey decided the bond that was needed there was for her to have a child with Merlin, but Merlin shunned sex. Morgan Le Fey's solution was to dose Merlin with one of her potions. Not only did Morgan Le Fey want her own son on the throne, she wanted to preserve the old ways. She and Arthur were both Celtic, and now, there was to be a son with Merlin.

When it became obvious that Morgan Le Fey was pregnant, she, again, refused to tell anyone who the father was. Since she and Merlin were both Celtic, Morgan Le Fey was willing to marry Merlin. It did not escape Merlin that his own bloodlines were close to what they would have needed to take the throne, but he did not want to marry Morgan Le Fey. Merlin knew Morgan Le Fey was being played by the opponents of Arthur who were going to support Mordred only long enough to get Arthur killed, and then raise public opinion against him as having killed his own father and resume their fighting over the throne.

Merlin thought that his son would be a more loving and balanced presence to have on the throne than Mordred.

Merlin decided he needed to be there to help his son grow up the way he wanted him to. Morgan Le Fey wanted Merlin to teach her more magic, and Merlin thought that was his only real opportunity to be near his son and raise him, instead of letting Morgaine fill him with her hatreds as she did to Mordred. Merlin, however, was going to need to drag this out over the many years it was going to take his son to grow up by being a reluctant teacher and by stressing that he had studied magic all of his life and that what he knew was no quick mastery of potions.

Merlin did not think he could go down, himself, there. He even thought that he could teach Morgan Le Fey in such a way that she would not be able to use it for her own power. When she pretended to be inept, Merlin even thought it did not matter what he taught her, but Morgan Le Fey practiced what she was learning, over and over, and became very good at it. After she gave birth, Morgan Le Fey did things to Merlin's son that he did not like. When she acted out her rage on his son, he tried to stop her, but she ignored him. Morgan Le Fey was intimidating with her rage, but Merlin did not leave because she had his son. Morgan Le Fey told Merlin she would not need to take her anger out on their son anymore if Merlin did not make her so angry by refusing to teach her what she wanted to know. This became a tool that Morgan Le Fey used to manipulate Merlin into teaching her things Merlin hadn't wanted her to know.

When Morgan Le Fey had learned all the magic she wanted to know, she was really done with Merlin. She lured Merlin into a cave, telling him she had put something there for him. The way she was acting, Merlin thought it might be his son and that he needed to rescue him. Merlin lost his center there, and did not analyze the situation. Morgan Le Fey trapped him in the cave, and simply told their son, with no explanation, that his father had gone away.

Morgan Le Fey was denied rage of Heart Daughter who wanted to take down Heart Son for being, in her perceptions, more important than her and for getting all the fanfare she wanted. She sought to get it through her denied Heart son,

Mordred, to make Heart Son into the man she wanted him to be and put him in the position she wanted him to have.

MY LIGHT KNOWS THE BALANCE POINT NOW

Although We didn't yet understand *The Unseen Role of Denial*, Our gap, the lost Will that was in it or the presence that Lucifer was therefore able to have, and even though the Mother, Heart and the Father of Manifestation each had a dominant role in the scenarios I just recounted, and even though My Loving Light, although not in manifested form, was present there and trying to help, it was not enough without the additional understandings We needed because I did not, yet, understand the Will or Its importance.

The Will is of crucial importance, as I have learned, and it was cruelly denied and judged against. We had so many denials of Our own in the beginning that We did not recognize the terribly serious imbalance this was causing in Creation, and We definitely didn't understand the role Our denials were playing or how they had become so turned against Us that there was no talking to or reasoning with them "out there."

I was so intent on denying My own rage as unloving that I did not recognize, for example, that the body who manifested was the rage polarization of Body. Instead, We tried to make it "work" and accept what We really didn't accept. Looking back, it is hard to believe that We tried to make Ourselves accept it when he guilt tripped Us so totally, playing on all of our insecurities and lack of self-acceptance in Ourselves, but when I looked around, no one else would come forward, so I thought I had to accept him. I wanted to manifest, and it didn't occur to Me that Body had completely intimidated the other parts of himself, so I tried to make the best of it. After all, he could manifest and was so certain where We were not.

It pains Me to have realized this, especially because of all the pain in Creation this has caused, but, I wasn't even sure then, that I was supposed to be God. Now I know what the problems in Creation are, and they are massive. This is why I said that I need your help to heal this. There is nowhere enough love in Creation. Unconditional love has become very confused with guilt. We originated this by trying to accept what We really didn't accept.

There was a time when I thought total destruction was the only solution, but now I am trying to heal this instead. I have seen that, in spite of it all, there is enough love in people to heal this. Most of the misery is a lack of self love. Religions have taught that love of self is wrong, but they are wrong. They have heard Lucifer and have been misled into believing it.

Body is Divine and a miracle of Creation, but religions have taught otherwise and Body has been treated as disposable. This is a massive misunderstanding that needs to be rectified now. There is Divine Body and a truly parental and guiding part of Body who is in the process of healing from what He experienced in His displacement.

What needs to be said now is that We must all heal together and lift Creation out of the mire of denial and confusion it's been in. I have finally figured out what has been wrong all this long time. It wasn't easy, but I have studied this enough that I am now certain that I'm right.

It is necessary to expand consciousness to be able to understand all of this as thoroughly as it needs to be understood. It is necessary to understand the gap and your own gapped presence in it enough to know what forms it has taken and what those forms you didn't think were you did there. When you get to the place where you are seeing the repeats in these forms and recognize their various patterns, I suggest that you let go of the forms these denials have taken in these places, releasing the judgments you have had there and staying as present as you can with the emotions there. Since reality is not a "given," this will allow the forms these denials have taken to go to their right place and shift into something that feels good. At the right time, which is when you are ready, this is the most expedient way to get healing.

Chances are, what you have not liked about "reality" and your life in it, is not reality the way it was meant to be. If you are moving and moving emotion and not understanding much more than you were, you are probably moving conversions and not the emotions that really need to move there, most likely terror that you are trapped in it with no way out, condemned to suffocate in dark compression. Suspect this, especially if your viewpoint is not shifting and opening into something wider and deeper. Suspect this if you still think your original viewpoint was so right that it is everything else that needs to change and shift until it comes into alignment with you.

From Our viewpoints, We have all thought that if We were only helped instead of opposed, Our viewpoint would have worked. We have all felt very wronged, but no one viewpoint would have worked, and there was no way to make it work. Fragmentation was already happening in Our earliest beginnings, even before there was light. I would have liked what happened later to have all been differentiation and emergence of Spirits, but in the gap, with little to no love present, it was fragmentation with judgments in the place of Loving Light. Now, to find balance requires going back over the situations in which parts of you fell away into denial, including the missing, not vibrating and seemingly dead pieces, until you can see how the pieces fit together, what they felt that polarized them and how that viewpoint has rightness that needs to be in its right place as a part of the whole picture.

Here are just some of the judgments that many have held: I forgive myself for the long held imprinted judgment that I cannot handle more consciousness, that what I have already is too much, not too little, that it was all overwhelming in the beginning and still is, that there's nothing I can do about it, that I wish I didn't even have to know about fear and other "negative" emotions, that once I go in there it's endless, that there's no saving myself, so why try, that it's hopeless, that the heartbreak is too big to heal, that I don't know how to help the situation or even myself and that there's not enough time for me to heal.

What you don't already know about how to fully heal, you are going to learn if you pay close attention while doing this process. Finding the balance point is your journey to full self-awareness that never took place in the beginning. No matter how it looks to you now, healing can be found if you have a loving heart, because that is where the balance point is going to be found. If your heart is shut down, feel that until you can open it. This balance point is going to feel good, and because you know it's right, you can sustain it instead of having guilt intrude on it. Because you will know how and why it was the way it was, you will not need to recreate it. Because you will know how to pay attention to all the subtle nuances and not get out ahead of them, fragments falling away in denial will not need to happen, and most of all, you will know that you have enough time to move at the speed that is right for you and still get where you want to be.

A STATE OF DENIAL THAT NEEDS HELP NOW

Now, I need to address sex, because most of you don't think you have been having sex in a state of denial anymore, but you really have been. The moment you go past anything, you are creating something that can go out in orgasm the way the secret agenda went out in blue. If you still have a gap, then gapped feelings are still going out and empowering the gap on Earth. They are doing this anyway, but not with the extra empowerment of the light generated in orgasm, especially if you are pressuring yourself to have sex or orgasm when you are not really feeling like that is what you want at the time.

There is a lot of sexual guilt that needs movement, as these gaps will testify, and having sex when you do not really want to is as much of a problem as not having sex when you really want to. The balance point here is something that needs to be found, and found soon, because empowering the gap is not really helping to get it off Earth.

I am not suggesting that you not have sex until your gap is healed, but I am suggesting that you move emotion as much as possible when you actually feel it and not later, when you "get to it," and especially during sex, when you think you don't have any. There is a lot of sexual rage that is not moving, except out, during orgasm, as held rage, and what it is doing is not pleasant to have to receive.

Feeling you deserve this is deeply imbedded in the subconscious of the people who have been receiving this unpleasant held rage, and this needs movement, too, to protect those who have feared saying "no" to this rage for fear of what it will do then. Self-denial came from this fear. The terror tactics used by this rage to get its own way need to move off of Earth now, too. To do this is not going to be easy, because this rage has not liked giving up the power positions anywhere that it has gone, and it has gone everyplace orgasms can go or push its way onto this planet.

Moving heartbreak helps, too. Many women still cry during sex and often don't know why, or think they do know why, but are not looking deeply enough, because they have not felt how much romantic heart and love's desire is not being met there or has been so backed up from the beginning. There is also terror that you are not going fast enough for the other person, aren't fulfilling their needs well enough, are sexually inadequate and are in danger of losing what little love and attention you do get from them in this way, but around this, sexual rage also needs movement, and there is rage; blaming rage and also just plain, primordial, sexual frustration and rage that may, or may not, blame the one you are having sex with at the time.

This is important, because not moving it puts punishment energy out there into the imprinting where it still believes it either needs to punish or 'deserves' punishment for what happened in the original split. If you tell yourself you are going to move it later, make sure you do, but in the moment is best. As you have more acceptance for yourself, it should be easier to find a place where this can happen without endangering your freedom at the hands of others who still would judge this.

Moving it in the moment is part of closing the gap between your feelings and when and how they are expressed. If you can't move it in the moment, move why this is so. Is it shame? Blue's interpretation of these feelings has a lot to do with this gap. Conditional love has been used by the upper chakras to make the lower chakras feel, well, "lower," and to not dare to be free or spontaneous.

Sex needs emotional movement, and right now, it is the most important area in which to move, because most people have more held emotion hidden in sexual activity than they have in motion. Yet, for the things that are still very gapped, I do not recommend using partners to act out on. I suggest continuing to do your movement in private, and even secrecy, until such time as you find yourself able to talk about it comfortably with those you trust before you move held sexual emotions with them. That is the best precaution and protection, and a necessary one at this time. Because most of the gap is sexually oriented, this is a large area to work on, and one which most of this book has tried to cover as best I can here.

Indigo has had to try to exist in the mess between Purple and Blue, but Indigo should not get lost in all of this, because Indigo has held the images of all of the nightmares as well as the good things about Creation.

Where the gap has been greater than the bond, Indigo has had a miserable existence and needs help in moving out the nightmare images that only the most gapped in unloving rage, mostly because it has been unmoving rage, have seemed to want to act out, yet this rage's own subjugated fear, terror and heartbreak have felt they have had no choice but to live them out. Lack of receptivity and terror tactics are the reasons for this. That is not fair, and it has been because those of us who originally polarized into rage, dumped it out, acted uninvolved, presented as only loving and let it go on.

Rage took the consciousness that was there and left. That is why I hold rage more responsible than fear and terror.

Rage also would not let fear and terror move in any way that could have gained the consciousness that was needed there; another reason why I hold rage more responsible. Rage also was dominant, abusive and acted out more than fear and terror for which rage must also take responsibility, but it also does need to be noticed and known that fear and terror did not know originally how it could let rage be there with it and find it to be a loving presence and, in disconnecting from it, also let it get out there with nothing to mitigate it.

Daughters have had something to offer here that can be found in the story of Beauty and the Beast, but do not think that is all there is to the picture, because they did not move their own rage there and pretended it was only the Beast who had it. In so doing, they portrayed themselves as having only the sweetness that fooled Me for so long, but it was easier for the daughters to seem to receive the fathers' rage because it was not really aimed at them, and at the level where they knew that, they did not mind letting it go where it was aimed, which was at the Mother. What the daughters do have to offer is the image of just letting sexual rage move.

The Mother has been so busy feeling blamed, taking all of the responsibility and alternately feeling like She is being unfairly blamed and not wanting to take so much responsibility, that She has often been very reactionary and defensive. When rage has approached Her, She has not been able to really listen to that rage enough to notice something that really needs to be noticed now about that rage.

That rage needs to be listened to for many reasons, but the one I want to point out now is that while there is a rage in the Will about My light not being present for it in all the ways I needed to be, there is another part of the rage that does not feel feminine. This is My rage, put into the Will long ago and not allowed to come back to Me until now. This rage does need to let Me know all of the judgments I made against the Will originally, but it also needs to move as sound, primordial sound, and come back to Me that way. It does not matter if it looks like a woman; this rage is not female. It is My light's rage that I wanted to blame on the Mother; so did Body, and so We pushed it into the Will, pounded it into the Will, in fact, and insisted it was the Will's rage. This rage felt it had no choice but to take on female form or, sometimes, Will male form that was rage polarized. Heart has been involved in this, too.

We have all given this rage trouble when it has tried to come back and not accepted it as Our own, because We all blamed the Mother as causing it when We felt judged and blamed by Her for not noticing Her when We needed to. We have all done a lot of perpetrating through this rage, too, and said it was the Mother. We need to take responsibility for that now, too.

The Mother does not know what Her response really is anymore without consciousness becoming more forthcoming about what it really knew, what it really knows and what it did not know, instead of just giving the old convenient answers of "I don't know" when it doesn't want to be bothered to know, or "I didn't know what I was doing" when it hasn't wanted to have to take responsibility. When She has been off base, We haven't helped Her to know what the balance point is because We have told Her everything that We haven't wanted to hear was off base. The Mother has been trying to take responsibility for this rage, feeling it must have been denied out of Her somehow, but it is not Her rage, and She does not have to take responsibility for it anymore.

We need to move along to accept Our own rage back. Just as big and unloving as it has looked to Us in the Mother there is just how much We feared the extent of Our rage and how much We judged it to be unloving and wanted to make it someone else's. We need to accept Her rage, too, but that is not the same thing as feeling Our rage that originated in Us, and that is important to notice.

Once you get through enough of the denials, blames, displacements, judgments and splits to bond more with each other, you will feel the difference between your own emotions and receiving someone else's. It feels good to receive someone else's emotions in a bond of love. It does not feel good to have them pounded in by someone else, told they are yours and be forced to hold them.

There have been form shifts for many reasons. As long as you are moving with what you need to be moving with, form shifts can take place when it is the right time for you in your own progression and in a way that you can find acceptable at the time.

Heartbreak was a major cause of this rage in males and needs to be looked at more as the lack of romantic heart presence than anything else right now, because it has not been moving as the large, emotionally held presence it really is. Rage has been too busy punishing the woman by withholding romantic heart and worse. The more a conversion into rage was placed on the heartbreak, the less romantic heart was allowed to be present and the more this fueled the sexual rage that needs to move in females.

This is necessary to know, because it is not a necessary place to stay in the emotional body. Rage and terror are too extreme to be handled well by the delicate beings We really are, and rage conversion has played a very causal role in making Us as dense as We have become. Rage punishment made terror increase and hold back. This contraction could not expand and cannot expand and open more space in which we can vibrate, unless it knows it is going to be safe. This balance needs to be found between the sexual partners involved, and is necessary in order to have sex that is not sex in a state of denial.

Heartbreak was felt on both sides, and this is where the bonding needs to take place from both sides so that the extremes of rage and terror can find balance. If you do not have much heart presence left, you may not be feeling heartbreak yet, but Heart is feeling it somewhere, and it is your heart, lost out there, that is feeling it. Lost heart pieces are out there in many places, not getting the help they need yet. Heart needs to be taken in between both parents and held there to feel where the balance point between the two really is.

Once heart feels the heartbreak moving between the parents, heart will be able to feel what the balance point really is, and then heart will be able to feel the polarities of rage and terror moving between the parents that heart needs to feel to be able to let it move through heart in the ways it needs to move to find the balance point there.

Heart needs to feel the terror in the Mother and the rage in the Father come to a balance point between the two in order to feel heart presence come to the balance point within itself. This is necessary to heal the problems We have had. Without full Heart presence, We do not have Our right place in which to balance. This is the gentling of the beast on both sides and is something that can be implemented now, even if it couldn't be then.

When you notice what your own flash point is, it is usually from not feeling received. Feeling received is a necessary part of love. It completes the full circle of giving out and receiving back when the reflection returns. We all need someplace to go with Our vibration, and that is what it is all about; giving Ourselves some place to go with Our vibration that really feels good. We all like to feel that We have someplace to go where We are received with love and without judgment; when that is real, that is a place that really feels good.

Life on Earth, now, has been looking pretty much like a frenetic distraction and avoidance of the original compression terror. If you sit down, or lie down, and attempt to relax, it is very likely you can reach only superficial layers of what is really going on inside of you. The bulk of most people's essence in these areas is unconscious and has been unconscious, basically, forever. People can often sense that something is there, but because of the gap, or space, have usually gone on to do something else, not knowing how to get to it or that it was important to get to it. This essence has managed to surface in various ways and forms at various times, also, usually unrecognized for what it is. Even without understanding it, however, the general feeling has become one of not being willing or able to go on this way anymore. This feeling has been arising from the presence of this essence which must be reached, helped and encouraged to vibrate and receive Loving Light this time. Since this essence has been unconscious, as it comes back to life, the agony in which it went unconscious is going to surface. It's going to be able to tell you what happened to it. Immense physical pain is likely to accompany intense emotions felt during the deaths this essence has drawn to try to show its plight. This is why I have said that this essence needs to be helped by being felt and helped to understand that it is going to be coming up out of torture and death with the help of loving acceptance, not beginning to stir only to go back down into what it has already been in forever. It can be very difficult to stay present through these deaths, but necessary. It is also necessary not to pressure yourself in ways that might actually result in your death. Staying present as long as you can and returning to it as soon as you can to make sure you are retrieving all of it will bring the healing needed to this lost Will.

By going to a private place, perhaps your bed when you are alone, and reaching for this essence by sinking into yourself, you can take your consciousness down into deep places within. Do not just look at it from your mind or with your third eye; actually be in it, put your consciousness in it, be present there with it and feel everything you can about it. Ask it to let you know what it has been holding and listen and receive it. You can begin by putting your consciousness into something easily reachable, such as one of your eyes or your nose or even your own brain, then progress to your neck and to whatever places in you are calling for your presence. If you find you are jumping out, return yourself. Then, put your consciousness in your upper back and Heart, and really feel what is going on in there. Put your consciousness into all of your chakras. The goal is to progress into bringing your consciousness into your entire body and into all of your essence.

As this is happening, many, many pictures and feelings can arise from this essence along with beliefs and imprints that it is not wanted, not allowed to live, not wanted to live, that it can only know suffering and death, that anything else is a trick to entice it forward to be tortured and killed again and so forth. The suffocation here is also very immense. Ask for My Loving Light to come in there and help so that all of these so long-held positions can be felt and helped to vibrate and open to receive Loving Light. When My Loving Light goes in there with you, it is going to help you to lift this essence, and it will feel easier to this essence to believe it can begin to vibrate so that it can open and receive Loving Light. Most of this essence has never had Loving Light come to it and offer to stay present with it. Any light it has had has been the unloving light of judgment. Give it importance because it is important, very important, to recover this essence now. This is how you can open more space in yourself for My Loving Light.

CONCLUSION

If you are ready and think you have had enough experience with the repetitions these imbalances have created, you can move along with My Loving Light now by doing the process I have brought to you in these books. My Light would like to have Its opportunity now because human potential needs to be reached.

You need to take all of yourself to healing, immortality and all of the other things you would really like to have, and there is no place for you to really do it like Earth. If you have a body, then that is what you have wanted to have for a long time, that is what you need to have and that is what you shall have. All of the hatred that has been pressuring against this possibility needs to move off of Earth, and that is a massive undertaking that needs as much movement as you can give it. You may feel yourself lost in swirling terror at times, but no matter how it looks now, it is going to be alright. Healing must happen, and healing is possible when you heal your Loving Heart.

The Light of My love is all Four Parts, Spirit, Will, Heart and Body, moving together in the true understanding and balance that is My Love; no more, no less.

If My Light is not coming down through the upper chakras in the right way, you cannot feel what it is meant to feel like and rise in the Will through the lower chakras to receive Me in the Heart in the ways you have always wanted to have it feel to you, which is not harsh like a shadeless drought or so intense that you cannot open your eyes in the daylight, but soft, loving and deliciously wonderful. It is the Will's colors rising to meet Me in the gentle pastels of a purple dawn, gentle breezes stirring in a beautiful, blue sky, morning like sunlight coming down through the green trees and subsiding with Me into the gentle golden evenings of the Will's deep colors when We need to rest; the Moon rising, first golden and then white, in the star sprinkled, Indigo night and flowing into the excitement of another pastel morning, colorfully rising, stirring you to return from your dreams, as you are nestled in the arms of romantic heart, to find them real and dance again with the Sun in the warm encouragement and rich abundance of a nurturing and colorful Earth that lets you know life is good and you can live it. There is music and excitement in the air! Can you hear and feel it yet?

And now, I would like to close with Amen, to that!

AMEN

INDIGO
The Search for True Understanding and Balance

is the eighth in a series of books channeled by Ceanne DeRohan

the books in the series are:

RIGHT USE OF WILL
Healing and Evolving the Emotional Body

ORIGINAL CAUSE I
The Unseen Role of Denial

ORIGINAL CAUSE II
The Reflection Lost Will Has to Give

EARTH SPELL
The Loss of Consciousness on Earth

HEART SONG
Vibrating Heartlessness to Let Heart In

LAND OF PAN
The Loss of Power and Magic on Earth

IMPRINTING
The Healing of the Chakras

INDIGO
The Search for True Understanding and Balance

These books need to be read in order. Getting ready for the sequels involves moving along with the material in Right Use of Will enough to know if this information is right for You. These books let you know your Original Cause by helping you access belief systems lost in the subconscious long ago, yet influencing your life every day. We appreciate that you have bought this book. If you are interested in others please visit our website: **https://www.rightuseofwill.com** or email us at: fourwindsbooks2@gmail.com. Thank you.

Four Winds Publications

www.ingramcontent.com/pod-product-compliance
Lightning Source LLC
Chambersburg PA
CBHW051123160426
43195CB00014B/2317